MATCHBOX®
TOYS 1948 TO 1993

DANA JOHNSON

COLLECTOR BOOKS
A Division of Schroeder Publishing Co., Inc.

The current values of this book should be used only as a guide. They are not intended to set prices, which vary from one section of the country to another. Auction prices as well as dealer prices vary and are affected by condition as well as demand. Neither the Author nor the Publisher assumes responsibility for any losses that might be incurred as a result of consulting this guide.

Although this book has been authorized by Tyco Toys, Inc. (parent company to Matchbox Toys), any errors or omissions are strictly the responsibility of the author.

Searching for a Publisher?

We are always looking for knowledgeable people considered to be experts within their fields. If you feel that there is a real need for a book on your collectible subject and have a large comprehensive collection, contact us.

Collector Books
P.O. Box 3009
Paducah, Kentucky 42002-3009

On the Cover:

Top row: **53 – D** Ford Zodiac with Superfast wheels/1970 $8.00; **44 – J** 1921 Ford Model T Van/1990 $2.00.
Second row: **K – 9 – D** Fire Tender/1973 $10.00; **Y – 09 – Ba** 1912 Simplex/1968 $30.00.
Bottom row: **K – 15 – B** The Londoner Bus "The Royal Wedding"/ 1981 $20.00; **10 – H** Buick LeSabre/1987 $3.00.

Cover design by Beth Summers
Book design by Terri Stalions and Timothy Scarbrough

Printed by IMAGE GRAPHICS, INC., Paducah, Kentucky

Dedicated to Ruth, who continues to support

my addiction to diecast toy vehicles.

TABLE OF CONTENTS ▬▬▬▬

About the Author 5
Acknowledgments 6

SECTION ONE: INTRODUCTION
   How to Use This Book 8
   Guide to Interpreting Values 9
   History of Matchbox Toys 10

SECTION TWO: NUMERICAL GUIDE TO CURRENT VALUES
   Early Lesney Toys 12
   1–75 Series Matchbox Miniatures 13
   40th Anniversary Collection & Matchbox Originals 37
   Gift Sets & Promotional Items 38
   The New Superfast 39
   Laser Wheels 40
   Lasertronics 40
   World Class 41
   Matchbox Preschool 41
   Super GT, Code II, Code III 42
   900 Series, Two Packs, Twin Packs & Trailer Series 42
   Convoy and Highway Express (Super Rigs 1993) 45
   Team Convoy, Team Matchbox & Convoy Action Packs 46
   "Days of Thunder" 46
   "Indy 500" Sets 46
   Sky Busters 47
   Major Pack Series 48
   King Size, Super Kings, & Speed Kings 49
   Action Series 57
   Matchbox Military & Battle Kings 57
   Sea Kings 58
   Adventure 2000 59
   Models of Yesteryear 59
   The Dinky Collection from Matchbox 63
   Catalogs 64

SECTION THREE: ILLUSTRATED GUIDE
   1-75 Series Matchbox Miniatures 70
   900 Series, Two Packs, Twin Packs, & Trailers 157
   Convoy Series, "Days of Thunder," & "Indy 500" 159
   King Size Series 162
   Sea Kings 176
   Sky Busters 177
   Models of Yesteryear 178
   Dinky Models 193
   Examples of Modern Packaging 193

SECTION FOUR: MATCHBOX MINIATURES 1-75 SERIES INDEX 194

ABOUT THE AUTHOR

Dana Johnson has collected and studied Matchbox toys since his family moved from the small town of Skandia in Michigan's Upper Peninsula to Lansing when he was seven. He recalls that at the age of ten he would ride his bike to a shopping center two miles from his home to spend his allowance on a 55¢ Matchbox toy from the dime store.

The prices of today's current models haven't changed much. You can still go to the local discount department store and pick up a Matchbox model for 99¢, but the models from the sixties are a different story. They now sell for $25 to $50, almost 100 times their original price.

In 1985 Dana moved to Bend, Oregon, where he now lives. His Matchbox collection has grown to over 600 models, still considered small by some avid collectors.

Meanwhile he has expanded his collecting to include diecast model vehicles made by Bburago, Corgi, Ertl, Hot Wheels, Lledo, Majorette, Politoy, Siku, Solido, Tomica, and others. He hopes to soon publish a similar collectors' guide to Majorettes, model vehicles made in France, which seem destined to be the next generation's collectible diecast toys. Selling for as low as 85¢, some models from the late eighties are already being offered by dealers for $10 or more.

While collecting these toys is a worthwhile investment, Dana mostly enjoys just looking at them and wondering why he finds such fascination for those colorful little cars.

ACKNOWLEDGMENTS

Thanks to Robert Goforth, Neil Waldmann of Neil's Wheels, and Lt. Col. James W. Smith for providing price lists and invaluable information on which values in this book are based; John Ridewood and Wendy Scott of Smick & Associates, Inc. for providing further reference material in the form of dealer catalogs; Patty Boyle and Robert LoMonaco of Tyco Toys for providing the latest literature on Matchbox and Tyco merchandise; to the hundreds of Matchbox enthusiasts who have supported this book through their purchases and letters. Special thanks to Claudia Valiquet for the idea and encouragement to publish this book. Photos by Chuck Lesowske.

The following are registered trademarks of Matchbox International Limited and Matchbox Toys U.S.A. Limited: MATCHBOX, SUPERFAST, LASER WHEELS, LASERTRONICS, LIGHTNING, WORLD CLASS, SUPER GT, TWO PACK, TWIN PACK, TRAILERS, CONVOY, HIGHWAY EXPRESS, TEAM CONVOY, TEAM MATCHBOX, SKY BUSTERS, MAJOR PACK, KING SIZE, SPEED KINGS, SUPER KINGS, MATCHBOX MILITARY, BATTLE KINGS, SEA KINGS, ADVENTURE 2000, SKYBUSTERS, MODELS OF YESTERYEAR, DINKY, ROLAMATICS, and others.

"DAYS OF THUNDER" is a copyrighted trademark licensed by Paramount Pictures. "INDY 500" and "INDIANAPOLIS 500" are licensed from IMS Corp. PETERBILT, KENWORTH, KW, and AERODYNE are licensed trademarks of Paccar, Inc., Bellevue, Washington. GOODYEAR is a trademark of Goodyear Tire and Rubber Company. JEEP is a trademark of the Chrysler Corporation. ROLLS ROYCE is a trademark of Rolls Royce, Ltd. CATERPILLAR and CAT are licensed trademarks of Caterpillar Tractor Company. Other trademarks used with permission. MATCHBOX is a registered trademark of Tyco Toys, Inc., used by permission.

SECTION ONE: INTRODUCTION ▬▬▬▬

HOW TO USE THIS BOOK ✪ GUIDE TO INTERPRETING VALUES ✪ HISTORY OF MATCHBOX TOYS

HOW TO USE THIS BOOK

This book is arranged in four sections: The Introduction, The Numerical Guide to Values, The Illustrated Guide, and The Matchbox Miniatures 1–75 Index.

The Introduction provides a background to this book, the history of Matchbox toys, and helps you to identify, date, and price models.

The Numerical Guide to Values is a current guide to values for the purpose of buying, selling, trading, and insuring your collection. Please remember that, because values vary from region to region, even collector to collector, this section is meant only as a guide.

The Illustrated Guide to Matchbox Miniatures features over 400 full-color plates of Matchbox Toys from the very latest to those cherished and very hard-to-find models collectors only dream of finding. It is an excellent visual aid for collectors and enthusiasts.

The Matchbox Miniatures 1–75 Index is an alphabetical listing by description, referenced to the **Numerical Guide of Values.** The author has endeavored to include every possible descriptive variation, so that you are more easily able to find the model in question when lacking model number or introduction year.

Major model changes are represented by successive letters added to the model number. 31 – A, for instance, represents the first model produced with the designated model number 31, the Ford Customline Station Wagon, introduced in 1957. 31 – G, in comparison, represents the seventh model produced with the designated number 31, Mazda RX-7, introduced in 1979.

Please note that some models have been issued under more than one model number or have been re-released with the same or different model number designation. It is not possible, therefore, to say with certainty that a certain model is discontinued. It can only be said that certain variations of a particular model may have been discontinued.

As an example, the Dodge Stake Truck, model number 4 – D, was first introduced in 1967. The addition of Superfast wheels in 1970 classifies this variation as a major model change, number 4 – E. In 1971 it was replaced by number 4 – F, Gruesome Twosome. The Dodge Stake Truck later reappeared in a Trailers set with the addition of a trailer and livestock.

1970 represents a significant year for matchbox models, as almost every model was converted to low-friction wheels and thin axles and designated Superfast. Even King Size models were renamed Super Kings.

In 1986 Superfast models were reintroduced as a set of 24 models with still different wheels than the other 1–75 models.

Models previously discontinued are still being reintroduced with color or other variations and number changes, sometimes in order to make more efficient use of older dies.

GUIDE TO INTERPRETING VALUES

Values mentioned in this book generally represent the highest value offered or requested for a given model. Although collectors are often willing to pay top dollar for models in mint condition in order to fill gaps in their collections, it is very likely that you will be able to purchase models for considerably less through the right seller. In the same spirit, if you intend to sell particular models in your collection, you will often need to lower the price in order to sell.

For standardization, all values mentioned in this book are for models in mint condition with original container. Deduct five percent if you don't have the original container. To help you determine the comparative value of a model in less than ideal condition, you may use the guide below.

For instance, if a model is valued at $75 in mint condition with original container, MOC, the same model in mint condition without the original container, M, may be valued around $71. The same model in very good condition, VG, is worth about $35 to $40. Phrases such as "may be," "about," and "around" are used to imply that prices are only approximations of what collectors generally are paying for such models. It is important to note, however, that the percentage value drops quickly as the condition of the model degrades. Models in less than what is considered "good" condition are essentially worthless. Also keep in mind that, although some collectors have done an excellent job of altering, customizing, or detailing models, this practice generally renders the model worthless and is, therefore, discouraged.

ABBREVIATIONS USED IN THIS BOOK

MOC	**M**int condition with **O**riginal **C**ontainer
M	**M**int condition without original container
NM	**N**ear **M**int condition; close inspection may show minute wear marks
EX	**EX**cellent condition; minor wear on edges
VG	**V**ery **G**ood; minor wear evident, decals or markings generally intact
G	**G**ood; overall wear evident, decals or markings partially missing
F	**F**air; excessive wear, decals may be generally worn off or markings noticeably worn off, parts and accessories generally intact
P	**P**oor; extreme wear, parts or accessories broken or missing

EFFECT OF CONDITION ON VALUE STATED IN THIS BOOK
Example: $75 value
Values rounded up to the nearest dollar

MOC	**100%** of stated value	$75
M	**95%** of stated value	$71
NM	**90%** of stated value	$68
EX	**70%** of stated value	$53
VG	**30%** of stated value	$23
G	**10%** of stated value	$8
F	**5%** of stated value	$4
P	**1%** of stated value	$1

HISTORY OF MATCHBOX TOYS

In 1947, two unrelated school friends, Rodney and Leslie Smith, started Lesney Products Company in a bombed-out London pub known as the Rifleman, with the intention of manufacturing diecast components for industrial applications.

In 1948, when production demands were low, Lesney started dabbling in toy manufacturing, introducing a wind-up tin elephant, a bait maker that forms bread into a small ball, and several model vehicles, some of which were later adapted to the Matchbox series. The popularity of these toys eventually dominated their production to the exclusion of anything else.

In 1952, Lesney introduced the large Coronation Coach in gold- and silver-colored versions measuring 15¾ inches long. The next year, the smaller version, 4½ inches long, was produced. Two hundred of the larger version were produced before the death of King George VI and feature figures of the King and Queen inside. When daughter Elizabeth II became heir to the throne, it was discovered that her husband Philip would not be riding with her, so the male figure was removed. About 32,800 more coaches were produced with this modification. The values of these first models now approach $1,000. The small coach was produced in much greater quantities and originally sold for about $1.25 U.S. Its popularity encouraged Rodney and Leslie to create the first three models of what would become the original Matchbox Series.

Starting with Number 1 Diesel Road Roller, Number 2 Dumper and Number 3 Cement Mixer, the 1–75 Matchbox Miniatures series was begun. The success of these first few models encouraged Leslie and Rodney to produce more models, eventually establishing the series of 75 different models in 1960.

John W. Odell, better known as Jack, provided the diecasting expertise. In the early 1980's, he left Matchbox to produce his own line of Lledo (Odell spelled backwards) toys, taking many of the original toy dies with him. Lledo remains the only toy company to produce diecast models still made in England.

Lesney Products continued its success through the 1960's, with the aid of marketing firms such as Moses Kohnstam (Moko), a company established near the turn of the century, and later Fred Bonner. But Lesney's success declined in the early 1970's due to increasing competition from Mattel in the form of Hot Wheels.

In 1983, Lesney sold the dies and rights to Universal International, a holding company based in Hong Kong. The parent company renamed its new subsidiary Matchbox Toys International with Matchbox Toys U.S.A. as its U.S. subsidiary based in Moonachie, New Jersey. By this time, many models were already being manufactured in Asia due to lower labor costs.

In 1987, Matchbox Toys purchased Dinky Toys, a name renowned in Europe since even before Matchbox, and produced a new line of Dinky Models, featuring much of the familiar style and detailing of the earlier Dinkys. The new line was featured in the 1989 Collector Catalog for the European market.

On October 2, 1992, Matchbox was again sold, this time to Tyco Toys, Inc. In comparison to Matchbox's multi-page collector catalogs of the past, Tyco's 1993 Collector Catalog is just a foldout sheet. King Size and Sky Busters are no longer marketed in the U.S., and Yesteryear and Dinky models are slated to be sold only through direct marketing to consumers from Matchbox's Australian division.

SECTION TWO: ━━━━━━
NUMERICAL GUIDE TO CURRENT VALUES

EARLY LESNEY TOYS ✵ 1-75 SERIES MATCHBOX MINIATURES

40TH ANNIVERSARY COLLECTION & MATCHBOX ORIGINALS

GIFT SETS & PROMOTIONAL ITEMS ✵ THE NEW SUPERFAST

LASER WHEELS ✵ LASERTRONICS ✵ WORLD CLASS ✵ MATCHBOX PRESCHOOL

SUPER GT'S, CODE II, CODE III ✵ 900 SERIES, TWO PACKS, TWIN PACKS, TRAILERS

CONVOY & HIGHWAY EXPRESS SERIES ✵ TEAM CONVOY, TEAM MATCHBOX & CONVOY ACTION PACKS

"DAYS OF THUNDER" ✵ "INDY 500"

SKYBUSTERS ✵ MAJOR PACK SERIES ✵ KING SIZE, SUPER KINGS & SPEED KINGS

ACTION SERIES: FARMING, CONSTRUCTION & EMERGENCY

MATCHBOX MILITARY & BATTLE KINGS ✵ SEA KINGS ✵ ADVENTURE 2000 ✵ MODELS OF YESTERYEAR

THE DINKY COLLECTION

CATALOGS

EARLY LESNEY TOYS ━━━━━━━━━━━━━━━

Lesney Products Company started manufacturing toys in 1948, a year after the company was begun. As industrial orders declined, Leslie and Rodney, with the help of their friend Jack Odell, started experimenting with the manufacture of diecast toys. Many of the early models created were later reproduced in miniature as the first of the Matchbox series. Here is a chronology of those early models.

YEAR INTRODUCED	DESCRIPTION	LENGTH	CURRENT VALUE
1948	Aveling Barford Diesel Road Roller	4⅜"	$450.00
	Caterpillar Bulldozer	4½"	$250.00
	Hand Cement Mixer	3⁹⁄₁₆"	$250.00
1949	Soap Box Racer	3⅛"	$400.00
	Rag and Bone Cart	5¼"	$500.00
	Caterpillar Tractor	3⅛"	$250.00
	Caterpillar Bulldozer	4½"	$250.00
	Ruston Bucyrus 10RB Excavator	4"	$500.00
	Horse Drawn Milk Cart	5⅜"	$250.00
1950	Prime Mover, Trailer, and Bulldozer Set	18"	$600.00
	Jumbo the Elephant (tin wind-up)	4"	$750.00
1951	Muffin the Mule (tin with moveable joints)	5½"	$300.00
1952	Large Coronation Coach	15¾"	$1,500.00
1953	Small Coronation Coach	4½"	$250.00
	Quarry Truck (prototype)	10"	$1,000.00
1954	Massey Harris Tractor	7¹³⁄₁₆"	$500.00
	Bread Bait Press	2"	$75.00
1955	Conestoga Wagon with 6 horses, barrels on sides	4⅞"	$250.00
	Conestoga Wagon with 6 horses, no barrels	4⅞"	$175.00

MATCHBOX MINIATURES 1–75 SERIES

From 1953 to the present, the mainstay of Matchbox toys has been the 1–75, or regular series, also referred to as Matchbox Miniatures. In 1969, most models were converted to what was then called "SuperFast," sporting thinner low-friction axles and wheels, in an effort to compete with Mattel Hot Wheels introduced in 1968.

In 1974 the Rolamatics were introduced — models with components that moved when rolled due to a pin on the inside of one or more wheels that activated various parts to move. The Badger has a rotating radar, the Stoat Armored Truck has a rotating lookout man, and the Beach Bouncer's driver bounces up and down.

The name "Lesney" last appeared on the base of Matchbox vehicles in 1982, as the Matchbox name was sold to Universal International, an Asian holding company. All models produced after 1982 are imprinted with either "MATCHBOX TOYS INTL" or "MATCHBOX INTL LTD." The value of Lesney-marked toys has risen notably since then.

Although Matchbox 1-75 series models are conveniently numbered, they are not consistent between U.S and European markets. The same model in each market often has a different number, and some models are only available in Europe, others only in the U.S. Through certain collectors and dealers, these European models can still be purchased in the U.S. This difference makes collecting and especially identifying models a bit more challenging, but still manageable. Please note this as you read this book. Also note that the abbreviation "SF" indicates SuperFast version. For more information on models in the 1–75 series, check the 1–75 Series Index beginning on page 194.

MODEL NUMBER	YEAR INTRODUCED	DESCRIPTION	LENGTH	CURRENT VALUE
1 – A	1953	Diesel Road Roller	1⅞"	$55.00
1 – B	1955	Road Roller	2¼"	$50.00
1 – C	1958	Road Roller	2⅜"	$45.00
1 – D	1962	Aveling Bedford Road Roller	2⅝"	$18.00
1 – E	1968	Mercedes Benz Lorry with regular wheels	3"	$15.00
1 – F	1970	Mercedes Benz Lorry with SF wheels	3"	$12.00
1 – G	1971	Mod Rod	2⅞"	$10.00
1 – H	1976	Dodge Challenger	2¹⁵/₁₆"	$8.00
1 – I	1982	Revin' Rebel Dodge Challenger	2⅞"	$6.00
1 – J	1983	Toyman Dodge Challenger	2⅞"	$4.00
1 – K	1987	Jaguar XJ6	3"	$2.00
1 – La	1988	Diesel Road Roller (green replica of 1 – A; CHINA)	1⅞"	$10.00
1 – Lb	1991	Diesel Road Roller (blue replica of 1 – A; CHINA)	1⅞"	$3.00
1 – M	1991	Jaguar XJ6 Police	3"	$4.00
1 – N	1993	Dodge Challenger "HEMI"	2⅞"	$2.00
2 – A	1953	Dumper	1⅝"	$60.00
2 – B	1957	Dumper	1⅞"	$50.00

MODEL NUMBER	YEAR INTRODUCED	DESCRIPTION	LENGTH	CURRENT VALUE
2 – C	1961	Muir Hill Dumper, "LAING"	2⅛"	$25.00
2 – D	1968	Mercedes Covered Trailer with regular wheels	3½"	$15.00
2 – E	1970	Mercedes Covered Trailer with SF wheels	3½"	$12.00
2 – F	1971	Jeep Hot Rod	2⁵⁄₁₆"	$10.00
2 – G	1976	Hovercraft	3⅛"	$8.00
2 – H	1981	S-2 Jet	2⅞"	$6.00
2 – I	1985	Pontiac Fiero	2¹³⁄₁₆"	$4.00
2 – J	1988	Rover Sterling	3"	$4.00
2 – K	1990	Corvette Grand Sport	3"	$2.00
3 – A	1953	Cement Mixer	1⅝"	$55.00
3 – B	1961	Bedford Ton Tipper	2½"	$30.00
3 – C	1968	Mercedes Benz Ambulance with regular wheels	2⅞"	$15.00
3 – D	1970	Mercedes Benz Ambulance with SF wheels	2⅞"	$12.00
3 – E	1973	Monteverdi Hai	2⅞"	$8.00
3 – Fa	1978	Porsche Turbo with LESNEY on base	3"	$6.00
3 – Fb	1983	Porsche Turbo with MATCHBOX INTL LTD on base	3"	$3.00
4 – A	1954	Massey Harris Tractor with fenders	1⅝"	$65.00
4 – B	1957	Massey Harris Tractor with no fenders	1⅝"	$60.00
4 – C	1960	Triumph Motorcycle and Sidecar	2⅛"	$50.00
4 – D	1967	Dodge Stake Truck with regular wheels	2⅞"	$15.00
4 – Ea	1970	Dodge Stake Truck with SF wheels and LESNEY on base	2¾"	$8.00
4 – Eb	1983	Dodge Stake Truck with MATCHBOX INTL LTD on base	2¾"	$3.00
4 – F	1971	Gruesome Twosome	2⅞"	$8.00
4 – G	1975	Pontiac Firebird	2⅞"	$5.00
4 – Ha	1979	1957 Chevy with LESNEY on base	2¹⁵⁄₁₆"	$5.00
4 – Hb	1983	1957 Chevy with MATCHBOX INTL LTD on base	2¹⁵⁄₁₆"	$2.00
4 – I	1987	Auston London Taxi (European model)	2⅝"	$4.00
4 – Ja	1988	Massey Harris Tractor (red replica of 4 – A; CHINA)	1⅝"	$10.00
4 – Jb	1991	Massey Harris Tractor (blue replica of 4 – A; CHINA)	1⅝"	$3.00
5 – A	1954	London Bus	2"	$60.00
5 – B	1957	London Bus	2¼"	$45.00
5 – C	1961	London Bus	2⁹⁄₁₆"	$35.00
5 – D	1965	London Bus	2¾"	$25.00

MODEL NUMBER	YEAR INTRODUCED	DESCRIPTION	LENGTH	CURRENT VALUE
5 – E	1969	Lotus Europa with SF wheels	2⅞"	$15.00
5 – F	1975	Seafire Boat	2¹⁵⁄₁₆"	$6.00
5 – G	1978	U.S. Mail Jeep	2⅜"	$6.00
5 – H	1982	4x4 Golden Eagle Off-Road Jeep	2⁷⁄₁₆"	$4.00
5 – I	1985	Peterbilt Petrol Tanker	3"	$3.00
5 – Ja	1988	London Bus (replica of 5 – A "BUY MATCHBOX SERIES")	2"	$10.00
5 – Jb	1991	London Bus (replica of 5 – A "MATCHBOX ORIGINALS")	2"	$3.00
6 – A	1954	Quarry Truck	2⅛"	$55.00
6 – B	1957	Euclid Quarry Truck	2½"	$50.00
6 – C	1964	Euclid Quarry Truck	2⅝"	$40.00
6 – D	1968	Ford Pickup with regular wheels	2¾"	$12.00
6 – E	1970	Ford Pickup with SF wheels	2¾"	$10.00
6 – F	1973	Mercedes 350SL Convertible	3"	$8.00
6 – G	1983	IMSA Mazda	3"	$4.00
6 – H	1985	F1 Racing Car (Europe; 16 – H/65 – G, U.S.)	2⅞"	$3.00
6 – I	1985	Ford Supervan (Europe; 72 – I, U.S.)	2¹⁵⁄₁₆"	$3.00
6 – J	1991	Alfa Romeo (Europe; 15 – L, U.S.)	2⅞"	$4.00
6 – K	1993	Quarry Truck (blue and gray replica of 6 – A)	2⅛"	$3.00
6 – L	1992	Excavator (prev. 32 – G)	3"	$2.00
7 – A	1954	Horse Drawn Milk Float with gray metal wheels	2¼"	$90.00
7 – B	1961	Ford Anglia	2⅝"	$45.00
7 – C	1966	Ford Refuse Truck with regular wheels	3"	$20.00
7 – D	1970	Ford Refuse Truck with SF wheels	3"	$8.00
7 – E	1971	Hairy Hustler	2⅞"	$6.00
7 – F	1976	Volkswagen Rabbit	2⅞"	$4.00
7 – G	1982	Volkswagen Rompin' Rabbit, 4 x 4	2⅞"	$4.00
7 – H	1983	Volkswagen Ruff Rabbit, 4 x 4	2⅞"	$4.00
7 – I	1983	IMSA Mazda (Europe; 6 – G, U.S.)	3"	$3.00
7 – J	1987	Porsche 959	2⅞"	$2.00
7 – Ka	1988	Horse Drawn Milk Float (orange replica of 7 – A)	2¼"	$10.00
7 – Kb	1991	Horse Drawn Milk Float (light blue replica of 7 – A)	2¼"	$3.00
7 – L	1993	T-Bird Stock Car	3"	$2.00
8 – A	1955	Caterpillar Tractor	1½"	$65.00
8 – B	1959	Caterpillar Tractor	1⅝"	$60.00

MODEL NUMBER	YEAR INTRODUCED	DESCRIPTION	LENGTH	CURRENT VALUE
8 – C	1961	Caterpillar Tractor	1⅞"	$55.00
8 – D	1964	Caterpillar Tractor	2"	$35.00
8 – E	1966	Ford Mustang Fastback with regular wheels	2⅞"	$16.00
8 – F	1970	Ford Mustang Fastback with SF wheels	2⅞"	$12.00
8 – G	1970	Ford Mustang Wildcat Dragster	2⅞"	$8.00
8 – H	1975	DeTomaso Pantera	3"	$5.00
8 – I	1982	Rover 3500 Police (European model)	3"	$8.00
8 – J	1983	Greased Lightning DeTomaso Pantera	3"	$4.00
8 – K	1986	Scania T142	3"	$3.00
8 – L	1987	Vauxhall Astra/Opel Kadett Police (European model)	2⅞"	$5.00
8 – M	1990	Mack CH600	3"	$2.00
8 – N	1992	Airport Fire Tender	3"	$2.00
9 – A	1955	Dennis Fire Escape with gray wheels	2¼"	$60.00
9 – B	1959	Merryweather Fire Engine	2½"	$30.00
9 – C	1966	Boat and Trailer with regular wheels	3¼"	$20.00
9 – D	1970	Boat and Trailer with SF wheels	3¼"	$6.00
9 – E	1971	AMX Javelin	3"	$6.00
9 – F	1978	Ford Escort RX2000	3"	$6.00
9 – G	1982	Fiat Abarth	2¹⁵⁄₁₆"	$5.00
9 – H	1983	Caterpillar Bulldozer	2⅝"	$4.00
9 – I	1987	Toyota MR2	2¾"	$4.00
9 – Ja	1988	Dennis Fire Escape (replica of 9 – A, red reels, "CHINA")	2¼"	$10.00
9 – K	1989	Faun Earth Mover Dump Truck (also see 53 – H and 58 –F)	3"	$2.00
9 – Jb	1991	Dennis Fire Escape (replica of 9 – A, yellow reels)	2¼"	$3.00
10 – A	1955	Mechanical Horse and Trailer	2⅜"	$65.00
10 – B	1958	Mechanical Horse and Trailer	1¹⁵⁄₁₆"	$55.00
10 – C	1961	Sugar Container Truck	2⅝"	$50.00
10 – D	1966	Leyland Pipe Truck with six pipes and regular wheels	2⅞"	$25.00
10 – E	1970	Leyland Pipe Truck with six pipes and SF wheels	2⅞"	$8.00
10 – F	1973	Mustang Piston Popper	2⅞"	$6.00
10 – G	1979	Plymouth Gran Fury Police	3"	$4.00
10 – H	1987	Buick LeSabre Stock Car	3"	$2.00
11 – A	1955	Road Tanker	2"	$55.00

MODEL NUMBER	YEAR INTRODUCED	DESCRIPTION	LENGTH	CURRENT VALUE
11 – B	1958	Road Tanker	2½"	$50.00
11 – C	1965	Taylor Jumbo Crane	3"	$18.00
11 – D	1969	Mercedes Benz Scaffold Truck with regular wheels	2½"	$15.00
11 – E	1969	Mercedes Benz Scaffold Truck with SF wheels	2½"	$8.00
11 – F	1972	Flying Bug	2⅞"	$6.00
11 – G	1976	Bedford Car Transporter	3"	$4.00
11 – H	1982	Mustang Cobra	2⅞"	$3.00
11 – I	1983	IMSA Mustang	3"	$3.00
11 – J	1985	Lamborghini Countach LP500S	3"	$3.00
12 – A	1955	Land Rover with driver	1¾"	$50.00
12 – B	1959	Land Rover without driver	2¼"	$40.00
12 – C	1965	Safari Land Rover with luggage on roof and regular wheels	2⅝"	$45.00
12 – D	1970	Safari Land Rover with luggage on roof and SF wheels	?	$15.00
12 – E	1970	Setra Coach	3"	$10.00
12 – F	1975	Big Bull Bulldozer	2⅜"	$5.00
12 – G	1979	Citroen CX Station Wagon	3"	$6.00
12 – H	1980	Citroen CX Ambulance (European model)	3"	$8.00
12 – I	1982	Pontiac Firebird S/E	3"	$5.00
12 – J	1986	Pontiac Firebird Racer	3"	$3.00
12 – K	1989	Modified Racer (see 32 – H)	2¹⁵/₁₆"	$3.00
12 – L	1990	Mercedes Benz 500SL Convertible	3"	$4.00
12 – M	1992	Dodge Cattle Truck	3"	$3.00
13 – A	1955	Bedford Wreck Truck	2"	$45.00
13 – B	1958	Bedford Wreck Truck	2⅛"	$40.00
13 – C	1961	Ford Thames Trader Wreck Truck	2½"	$45.00
13 – D	1965	Dodge Wreck Truck, "BP," with regular wheels	3"	$24.00
13 – E	1970	Dodge Wreck Truck, "BP," with SF wheels	3"	$12.00
13 – F	1971	Baja Dune Buggy	2⅝"	$10.00
13 – G	1977	Snorkel Fire Engine with closed cab	3"	$6.00
13 – H	1982	4x4 Mini-Pickup with roll bar and rally lights (Dunes Racer)	2¾"	$4.00
13 – I	1983	4x4 Mini-Pickup with roof foil	2¾"	$4.00
13 – J	1993	Bedford Wreck Truck (replica of 13 – A)	2"	$3.00
14 – A	1956	Daimler Ambulance	1⅞"	$55.00

MODEL NUMBER	YEAR INTRODUCED	DESCRIPTION	LENGTH	CURRENT VALUE
14 – B	1958	Daimler Ambulance	2⅝"	$50.00
14 – C	1962	Bedford Lomas Ambulance	2⅝"	$40.00
14 – D	1968	Iso Grifo with chrome hubs	3"	$20.00
14 – E	1969	Iso Grifo with SF wheels	3"	$8.00
14 – F	1973	Rallye Royale	2⅞"	$8.00
14 – G	1975	Mini HaHa Mini Cooper	2⅜"	$6.00
14 – H	1982	Leyland Tanker (European model)	3⅛"	$20.00
14 – I	1983	1983 Corvette Convertible	3"	$5.00
14 – J	1984	1984 Corvette Convertible	3"	$3.00
14 – K	1987	Jeep Eagle/Laredo	2⅝"	$4.00
14 – L	1987	1987 Corvette Convertible	3"	$2.00
14 – M	1988	1988 Corvette Convertible	3"	$2.00
14 – N	1989	Grand Prix Racer	3"	$2.00
15 – A	1956	Prime Mover Truck Tractor	2⅛"	$45.00
15 – B	1959	Atlantic Super Truck Tractor	2⅝"	$40.00
15 – C	1963	Dennis Refuse Truck "CLEANSING SERVICE"	2½"	$30.00
15 – D	1968	Volkswagen 1500 Saloon with chrome hubs	2⅞"	$20.00
15 – E	1970	Volkswagen 1500 Saloon with SF wheels	2⅞"	$8.00
15 – F	1971	Hi Ho Silver! Volkswagen	2½"	$6.00
15 – G	1972	Ford Lift Truck	2½"	$5.00
15 – H	1983	Ford Sierra XR4Ti	3"	$4.00
15 – I	1984	Ford Sierra XR4Ti	3"	$4.00
15 – J	1985	Peugeot 205 Turbo 16 (European model)	2¹¹⁄₁₆"	$6.00
15 – K	1988	Saab 9000	3"	$4.00
15 – L	1990	Corvette Grand Sport	3"	$2.00
15 – M	1991	Alfa Romeo	2⅞"	$2.00
15 – N	1992	Sunburner (Dodge Viper)	3"	$2.00
16 – A	1956	Atlantic Trailer	3⅛"	$40.00
16 – B	1957	Atlantic Trailer	3¼"	$30.00
16 – C	1964	Scammell Mountaineer Dump Truck with plow	2¾"	$75.00
16 – D	1969	Case Tractor Bulldozer	2½"	$45.00
16 – E	1974	Badger Exploration Truck with Rolamatic radar	2⅞"	$12.00
16 – F	1979	Pontiac Firebird Trans Am	3"	$4.00
16 – G	1982	Pontiac Trans Am	3"	$4.00

MODEL NUMBER	YEAR INTRODUCED	DESCRIPTION	LENGTH	CURRENT VALUE
16 – H	1984	Formula Racer "PIRELLI"	3"	$4.00
16 – I	1985	Pontiac Trans Am T-Roof	3"	$3.00
16 – J	1990	Ford LTD Police	3"	$2.00
16 – K	1990	Land Rover Ninety (Europe; 35 – H, U.S.)	2½"	$2.00
17 – A	1956	Bedford Van "MATCHBOX REMOVAL SERVICE"	2⅛"	$50.00
17 – B	1960	Austin London Taxi	2¼"	$45.00
17 – C	1963	Hoveringham Tipper	2⅞"	$35.00
17 – D	1969	AEC Ergomatic Cab Horse Box with regular wheels	2¾"	$20.00
17 – E	1970	AEC Ergomatic Cab Horse Box with SF wheels	2¾"	$12.00
17 – F	1972	London Bus with small windows	3"	$15.00
17 – G	1982	London Bus with large windows	3"	$10.00
17 – H	1983	AMX Pro Stocker	2⅝"	$6.00
17 – I	1985	Ford Escort XR31 Cabriolet	2¾"	$4.00
17 – J	1990	Dodge Dakota Pickup	3"	$3.00
18 – A	1956	Caterpillar D8 Bulldozer with blade	1⅞"	$40.00
18 – B	1958	Caterpillar D8 Bulldozer with no braces on blade	2"	$35.00
18 – C	1961	Caterpillar D8 Bulldozer with braces on blade	2¼"	$33.00
18 – D	1964	Caterpillar Crawler	2⅜"	$30.00
18 – E	1969	Field Car with tires on plastic hubs	2⅝"	$25.00
18 – F	1970	Field Car with SF wheels	2⅝"	$10.00
18 – G	1975	Hondarora Harley Davidson Motorcycle and rider	2⅜"	$8.00
18 – H	1984	Extending Ladder Fire Engine	3"	$3.00
19 – A	1956	MG Midget Sports Car with driver	2"	$50.00
19 – B	1958	MGA Sports Car	2¼"	$45.00
19 – C	1961	Aston Martin Racing Car	2½"	$40.00
19 – Da	1966	Lotus Racing Car with spoked wheels	2¾"	$30.00
19 – Db	1966	Lotus Racing Car with tires on plastic hubs	2¾"	$28.00
19 – E	1970	Lotus Racing Car with SF wheels	2¾"	$15.00
19 – F	1970	Road Dragster	2⅞"	$8.00
19 – G	1976	Badger Cement Truck	3"	$6.00
19 – H	1982	Peterbilt Cement Truck	3"	$5.00
19 – I	1993	MG Midget Sports Car (replica of 19 – A)	2"	$3.00

MODEL NUMBER	YEAR INTRODUCED	DESCRIPTION	LENGTH	CURRENT VALUE
20 – A	1956	Stake Truck	2⅜"	$40.00
20 – B	1959	ERF 686 Truck "EVEREADY FOR LIFE"	2⅝"	$36.00
20 – C	1965	Chevrolet Impala Taxi with driver	3"	$32.00
20 – D	1969	Lamborghini Marzal with SF wheels	2¾"	$12.00
20 – E	1975	Range Rover Police Patrol with Rolamatic	2⅞"	$6.00
20 – F	1982	Desert Dawg 4x4 Jeep	2⅝"	$4.00
20 – G	1983	Jeep Laredo/Eagle 4x4	2⅝"	$4.00
20 – H	1985	Jeep Laredo/Eagle 4x4	2⁷⁄₁₆"	$4.00
20 – I	1986	Volvo Container Truck	3"	$3.00
20 – J	1988	Volkswagen Ambulance Vanagon	2⅞"	$3.00
21 – A	1956	Bedford Duplé Long Distance Coach	2¼"	$55.00
21 – B	1958	Bedford Duplé Long Distance Coach	2⅝"	$45.00
21 – C	1961	Commer Milk Truck	2¼"	$35.00
21 – D	1968	Foden Concrete Truck with regular wheels	2⅞"	$25.00
21 – E	1970	Foden Concrete Truck with SF wheels	2⅞"	$15.00
21 – F	1973	Rod Roller	2⅝"	$8.00
21 – G	1978	Renault 5TL	2¹¹⁄₁₆"	$10.00
21 – H	1983	Corvette Pace Car	3"	$4.00
21 – I	1986	Breakdown Van	3"	$3.00
21 – J	1987	GMC Wreck Truck	2⅞"	$2.00
21 – K	1991	Nissan Prairie	2⅞"	$2.00
22 – A	1956	Vauxhall Cresta Sedan	2½"	$45.00
22 – B	1955	Vauxhall Cresta Sedan with windows	2⅝"	$36.00
22 – C	1964	Pontiac Grand Prix with regular wheels and opening doors	3"	$18.00
22 – D	1970	Pontiac Grand Prix with SF wheels	3"	$12.00
22 – E	1970	Freeman Inter-City Commuter Coach	3"	$8.00
22 – F	1975	Blaze Buster Fire Engine	3"	$6.00
22 – Ga	1982	Toyota Mini Pickup Camper	2¾"	$4.00
22 – Gb	1983	Bigfoot Toyota Mini Pickup Camper	2¾"	$4.00
22 – H	1984	Jaguar XK120	3"	$3.00
22 – I	1989	Saab 9000	2¹⁵⁄₁₆"	$2.00
22 – J	1990	Opel Vectra/Chevrolet Cavalier GS	3"	$2.00
22 – K	1992	Lamborghini Diablo	3"	$2.00

MODEL NUMBER	YEAR INTRODUCED	DESCRIPTION	LENGTH	CURRENT VALUE
23 – A	1956	Berkeley Cavalier Travel Trailer	2½"	$40.00
23 – B	1960	Bluebird Dauphine Travel Trailer	2½"	$32.00
23 – C	1965	Trailer Caravan	2⅞"	$20.00
23 – D	1970	Volkswagen Camper with opening roof	2⅛"	$10.00
23 – E	1975	Atlas Truck	3"	$4.00
23 – F	1979	Mustang GT350	2⅞"	$4.00
23 – G	1982	Audi Quattro	3"	$3.00
23 – H	1982	Peterbilt Tipper	3"	$3.00
23 – I	1985	Volvo Container Truck	3"	$3.00
24 – A	1956	Weatherhill Hydraulic Excavator	2⅜"	$40.00
24 – B	1959	Weatherhill Hydraulic Excavator	2⅝"	$35.00
24 – C	1967	Rolls Royce Silver Shadow with chrome hubs	3"	$16.00
24 – D	1970	Rolls Royce Silver Shadow with SF wheels	3"	$6.00
24 – E	1973	Team Matchbox Formula 1 Racer	2⅞"	$6.00
24 – F	1978	Diesel Shunter	3"	$4.00
24 – G	1982	Datsun 280ZX	3"	$2.00
24 – H	1983	Datsun 280ZX 2+2	3"	$2.00
24 – I	1987	Nissan 300ZX Turbo	2⅞"	$2.00
24 – J	1989	Ferrari F40	3"	$2.00
24 – K	1990	Lincoln Town Car	3"	$2.00
24 – L	1992	Airport Fire Tender	3"	$2.00
25 – A	1956	Bedford 12CWT "DUNLOP" Van	2⅛"	$50.00
25 – B	1960	Volkswagen 1200 Sedan	2½"	$35.00
25 – C	1964	Bedford Petrol Tanker with tilt cab	3"	$30.00
25 – D	1968	Ford Cortina GT with regular wheels	2⅞"	$20.00
25 – E	1970	Ford Cortina GT with SF wheels	2⅝"	$8.00
25 – F	1972	Mod Tractor	2⅛"	$6.00
25 – G	1978	Flat Car with container	3"	$4.00
25 – H	1978	Toyota Celica GT	2¹⁵⁄₁₆"	$4.00
25 – I	1982	Toyota Celica GT with oversized rear wheels	2¹⁵⁄₁₆"	$4.00
25 – J	1982	Audi Quattro	3"	$3.00
25 – K	1983	Chevrolet Ambulance (see 41 – E, 1978)	2¹⁵⁄₁₆"	$3.00
25 – L	1985	Peugeot Quasar (see 49 – H)	2¾"	$2.00

MODEL NUMBER	YEAR INTRODUCED	DESCRIPTION	LENGTH	CURRENT VALUE
26 – A	1956	Foden Ready Mix Concrete Truck	1¾"	$65.00
26 – B	1961	Foden Ready Mix Concrete Truck	2½"	$50.00
26 – C	1968	GMC Tipper Truck with regular wheels	2⅝"	$25.00
26 – D	1970	GMC Tipper Truck with SF wheels	2⅝"	$10.00
26 – E	1972	Big Banger (later model 26 – G, Cosmic Blues)	3"	$8.00
26 – F	1976	Site Dumper	2⅝"	$4.00
26 – Ga	1980	Cosmic Blues, white with blue accents	3"	$4.00
26 – Gb	1980	Cosmic Blues, blue with white accents	3"	$2.00
26 – H	1984	Volvo Covered Tilt Truck	3"	$2.00
26 – I	1984	Volvo Cable Truck (rare variation of 23 – I)	3"	$15.00
26 – J	1989	BMW 5-Series 535i	3"	$2.00
26 – K	1993	Foden Ready Mix Concrete Truck (replica of 26 – A)	2½"	$3.00
26 – L	1993	Chevy Van	3"	$2.00
27 – A	1956	Bedford Low Loader	1⅜"	$120.00
27 – B	1959	Bedford Low Loader	3¾"	$60.00
27 – C	1960	Cadillac Sixty Special	2¾"	$50.00
27 – D	1966	Mercedes Benz 230SL Convertible with regular wheels	3"	$25.00
27 – E	1970	Mercedes Benz 230SL Convertible with SF wheels	2⅞"	$15.00
27 – F	1973	Lamborghini Countach with opening rear cowl	2⅞"	$8.00
27 – G	1981	Swing Wing Jet	3"	$4.00
27 – H	1987	Jeep Cherokee	2⅞"	$2.00
27 – I	1991	Mercedes Benz 1600 Turbo Tractor	2¾"	$2.00
28 – A	1956	Bedford Compressor Truck	2¼"	$50.00
28 – B	1959	Thames Trader Compressor Truck	2¾"	$40.00
28 – C	1964	Mark 10 Jaguar	2¾"	$25.00
28 – D	1968	Mack Dump Truck with regular wheels	2⅝"	$20.00
28 – E	1970	Mack Dump Truck with SF wheels	2⅝"	$10.00
28 – F	1974	Stoat Armored Truck	2⅝"	$8.00
28 – G	1979	Lincoln Continental Mark V	3"	$4.00
28 – H	1982	Formula Racing Car	3⅛"	$2.00
28 – I	1984	1984 Dodge Daytona Turbo Z	2⅞"	$2.00
28 – J	1988	T-Bird Turbo Coupe	3"	$2.00
28 – K	1990	Leyland Titan London Bus (see 17 – F)	3"	$3.00
28 – L	1990	Corvette Convertible	3"	$2.00
28 – M	1991	Fork Lift Truck	3"	$2.00

MODEL NUMBER	YEAR INTRODUCED	DESCRIPTION	LENGTH	CURRENT VALUE
29 – A	1956	Bedford Milk Delivery Van	2¼"	$40.00
29 – B	1961	Austin A55 Cambridge	2¾"	$36.00
29 – C	1966	Fire Pumper with regular wheels	3"	$20.00
29 – D	1970	Fire Pumper with SF wheels	3"	$8.00
29 – E	1970	Racing Mini	2¼"	$6.00
29 – F	1976	Shovel Nose Tractor	2⅞"	$3.00
30 – A	1956	Ford Prefect	2¼"	$45.00
30 – B	1961	6-Wheel Crane Truck	2⅝"	$36.00
30 – C	1965	8-Wheel Crane Truck with regular wheels	3"	$20.00
30 – D	1970	8-Wheel Crane Truck with SF wheels	3"	$12.00
30 – E	1971	Beach Buggy	2⅝"	$12.00
30 – F	1976	Swamp Rat	3"	$6.00
30 – G	1981	Leyland Articulated Truck	3"	$20.00
30 – H	1982	Peterbilt Quarry Truck	3"	$6.00
30 – I	1984	Mercedes Benz 280GE G-Wagon	3"	$4.00
31 – A	1957	Ford Customline Station Wagon	2¾"	$45.00
31 – B	1960	Ford Fairlane Station Wagon	2¾"	$40.00
31 – C	1964	Lincoln Continental with regular wheels	2¾"	$25.00
31 – D	1969	Lincoln Continental with SF wheels	2¾"	$12.00
31 – E	1971	Volks Dragon	2½"	$8.00
31 – F	1977	Caravan Travel Trailer	2¹¹⁄₁₆"	$4.00
31 – G	1979	Mazda Savannah RX-7 without spoiler	3"	$4.00
31 – H	1982	Mazda Savannah RX-7 with spoiler	3"	$4.00
31 – I	1987	Rolls Royce Silver Cloud (Europe; 62 – G, U.S.)	3"	$3.00
31 – J	1988	Rover Sterling	2¹⁵⁄₁₆"	$3.00
31 – K	1990	BMW-5 Series 535i	3"	$2.00
31 – L	1991	Nissan Prairie	2⅞"	$2.00
31 – M	1993	Jaguar XJ220	3⅛"	$2.00
32 – A	1957	Jaguar XK140 Coupe	2⅜"	$50.00
32 – B	1962	Jaguar XKE with clear plastic windows	2⅝"	$40.00
32 – C	1968	Leyland Petrol Tanker with regular wheels	3"	$16.00
32 – D	1970	Leyland Petrol Tanker with SF wheels	3"	$10.00
32 – E	1972	Maserati Bora	3"	$8.00

MODEL NUMBER	YEAR INTRODUCED	DESCRIPTION	LENGTH	CURRENT VALUE
32 – F	1978	Field Gun	3"	$5.00
32 – G	1981	Atlas Excavator	3"	$3.00
32 – H	1990	Modified Racer	2¹⁵⁄₁₆"	$2.00
32 – I	1993	Jaguar XK140 Coupe (replica of 32 – A)	2⅜"	$3.00
33 – A	1957	Ford Zodiac	2⅝"	$50.00
33 – B	1963	Ford Zephyr 6 Mk III	2⅝"	$30.00
33 – C	1969	Lamborghini Miura with chrome hubs	2¾"	$20.00
33 – D	1970	Lamborghini Miura with SF wheels	2¾"	$12.00
33 – E	1973	Datsun 126X	3"	$6.00
33 – F	1977	Police Motorcyclist Honda CB750	2½"	$6.00
33 – G	1986	Volkswagen Golf GTi	2⅞"	$4.00
33 – H	1987	Renault 11 Alliance	2¹⁵⁄₁₆"	$2.00
33 – I	1988	Mercury Sable Wagon	3"	$2.00
33 – J	1989	Ford Utility Truck	3"	$2.00
33 – K	1990	Mercedes Benz 500SL Convertible (Europe; 12 – L, U.S.)	3"	$2.00
34 – A	1957	Volkswagen Van "MATCHBOX EXPRESS"	2¼"	$55.00
34 – B	1962	Volkswagen Camper, light green	2¾"	$50.00
34 – C	1967	Volkswagen Camper, silver with raised roof	2⅝"	$50.00
34 – D	1968	Volkswagen Camper, silver with low roof	2⅝"	$45.00
34 – E	1971	Formula One Racing Car	2⅞"	$6.00
34 – F	1975	Vantastic	2⅞"	$6.00
34 – G	1981	Chevy Pro Stocker	3"	$4.00
34 – H	1983	Toyman Dodge Challenger	3"	$3.00
34 – I	1986	Chevy Pro Stocker Halley's Comet Car	3"	$6.00
34 – J	1987	Ford RS200	2⅞"	$4.00
34 – K	1990	Sprint Racer	2¹⁵⁄₁₆"	$2.00
35 – A	1957	Marshall Horse Box	2"	$55.00
35 – B	1964	Snow Trac Tractor	2⅜"	$45.00
35 – C	1969	Merryweather Fire Engine (SF only)	3"	$15.00
35 – D	1975	Fandango	3"	$8.00
35 – E	1981	Volvo Zoo Truck (rare variation of 23 – I)	3"	$20.00
35 – F	1982	Trans Am T-Roof	3"	$6.00
35 – G	1986	4x4 Pickup Camper	3"	$3.00

MODEL NUMBER	YEAR INTRODUCED	DESCRIPTION	LENGTH	CURRENT VALUE
35 – H	1989	Ford Bronco II (also see 39 – H)	3"	$2.00
35 – I	1990	Land Rover Ninety (also 16 – K)	2½"	$2.00
35 – J	1993	Pontiac Stock Car	3"	$2.00
36 – A	1957	Austin A50 Sedan	2⅝"	$45.00
36 – B	1961	Lambretta TV175 Scooter and Sidecar	2"	$40.00
36 – C	1966	Opel Diplomat with regular wheels	2⅞"	$15.00
36 – D	1970	Opel Diplomat with SF wheels	2⅞"	$10.00
36 – E	1970	Hot Rod Draguar	2¹³⁄₁₆"	$6.00
36 – F	1975	Formula 5000	3"	$6.00
36 – G	1980	Refuse Truck	3"	$4.00
37 – A	1957	Coca-Cola Lorry with uneven cases and metal wheels	2¼"	$75.00
37 – B	1957	Coca-Cola Lorry with even cases and metal wheels	2¼"	$55.00
37 – C	1960	Coca-Cola Lorry with even cases and plastic wheels	2¼"	$35.00
37 – D	1966	Dodge Cattle Truck with regular wheels	2½"	$25.00
37 – E	1970	Dodge Cattle Truck with SF wheels	2½"	$10.00
37 – F	1972	Soopa Coopa	2⅞"	$6.00
37 – G	1976	Skip Truck	2¹¹⁄₁₆"	$6.00
37 – H	1982	Maserati Bora Sunburner	3"	$4.00
37 – I	1982	Matra Rancho (European model)	2⅞"	$12.00
37 – J	1984	Jeep 4x4 with roll cage and winch	2⅞"	$4.00
37 – K	1986	Ford Escort XR3i Cabriolet	2⅞"	$3.00
37 – L	1991	Nissan 300ZX	3"	$2.00
37 – M	1992	Mercedes Benz 600SL (also 38 – J)	3"	$2.00
38 – A	1957	Karrier Refuse Truck	2⅜"	$45.00
38 – B	1963	Vauxhall Victor Estate Car	2⅝"	$35.00
38 – C	1967	Honda Motorcycle and Trailer with regular wheels	2⅞"	$25.00
38 – D	1970	Honda Motorcycle and Trailer with SF wheels	2⅞"	$10.00
38 – E	1973	Stingeroo Cycle (3-wheel motorcycle)	3"	$6.00
38 – F	1976	Jeep (with or without top)	2⅜"	$8.00
38 – G	1980	Camper Pickup Truck	3"	$12.00
38 – H	1982	Model A Truck (many variations)	3"	$10.00
38 – I	1992	Ford Courier	3"	$2.00
38 – J	1992	Mercedes 600SL (also 37 – M)	3"	$2.00

MODEL NUMBER	YEAR INTRODUCED	DESCRIPTION	LENGTH	CURRENT VALUE
39 – A	1957	Ford Zodiac Convertible	2⅝"	$50.00
39 – B	1962	Pontiac Convertible	2¾"	$45.00
39 – C	1967	Ford Tractor	2⅛"	$20.00
39 – D	1973	Clipper with opening cockpit	3"	$8.00
39 – E	1979	Rolls Royce Silver Shadow II	3¹⁄₁₆"	$8.00
39 – F	1982	Toyota Celica Supra	3"	$6.00
39 – G	1985	BMW 323i Cabriolet	2¾"	$4.00
39 – H	1990	Ford Bronco II 4x4	3"	$2.00
39 – I	1990	Mack CH600 (see 8 – M)	3"	$2.00
39 – J	1991	Mercedes Benz 600SEL (see 37 – M)	3"	$2.00
40 – A	1957	Bedford Tipper Truck	2⅛"	$35.00
40 – B	1961	Leyland Royal Tiger Coach	3"	$25.00
40 – C	1967	Hay Trailer	3¼"	$15.00
40 – D	1971	Vauxhall Guildsman with SF only	3"	$15.00
40 – E	1977	Bedford Horse Box with two horses	2¹³⁄₁₆"	$8.00
40 – F	1982	Corvette T-Roof	3"	$4.00
40 – G	1983	Sierra XR4Ti (also see 15 –H and 55 – N)	3"	$2.00
40 – H	1985	NASA Rocket Transporter	3"	$2.00
40 – I	1991	Road Roller	3"	$2.00
41 – A	1957	D-Type Jaguar	2³⁄₁₆"	$50.00
41 – B	1960	D-Type Jaguar (tires will separate from hubs)	2⁷⁄₁₆"	$45.00
41 – C	1965	Ford GT (tires will separate from hubs)	2⅝"	$25.00
41 – D	1970	Ford GT with SF wheels	2⅝"	$12.00
41 – E	1972	Siva Spider	3"	$8.00
41 – F	1978	Chevrolet Ambulance (see 25 – J)	2¹⁵⁄₁₆"	$4.00
41 – G	1982	Kenworth Conventional Aerodyne	2¾"	$2.00
41 – H	1983	Racing Porsche	3"	$2.00
41 – I	1987	Jaguar XJ6	3"	$2.00
41 – J	1991	Opel Vectra/Cavalier	3"	$2.00
41 – K	1992	Sunburner	3"	$2.00
41 – L	1993	Cosmic Blues "HEMI" (also 26 – G)	3"	$2.00
42 – A	1957	Bedford Van "EVENING NEWS"	2¼"	$50.00
42 – B	1965	Studebaker Wagonaire with hunter and two dogs	3"	$25.00
42 – C	1969	Iron Fairy Crane with regular wheels	3"	$40.00

MODEL NUMBER	YEAR INTRODUCED	DESCRIPTION	LENGTH	CURRENT VALUE
42 – D	1970	Iron Fairy Crane with SF wheels	3"	$20.00
42 – E	1972	Tyre Fryer	3"	$6.00
42 – F	1977	Mercedes Container Truck	3"	$6.00
42 – G	1982	1957 T-Bird	3"	$4.00
42 – H	1985	Faun Mobile Crane	3"	$2.00
43 – A	1958	Hillman Minx Sedan	2⅝"	$40.00
43 – B	1962	Aveling Barford Tractor Shovel	2⅝"	$40.00
43 – C	1968	Pony Trailer with two horses and regular wheels	2⅝"	$20.00
43 – D	1970	Pony Trailer with two horses and SF wheels	2⅝"	$10.00
43 – E	1972	Dragon Wheels	2¹³⁄₁₆"	$6.00
43 – F	1978	0-4-0 Steam Locomotive	3"	$10.00
43 – G	1979	1957 Chevy	3"	$2.00
43 – H	1982	Peterbilt Conventional	2¾"	$12.00
43 – I	1984	AMG Mercedes Benz 500SEC	2⅞"	$6.00
43 – J	1987	Renault 11 Turbo Alliance	2¾"	$2.00
43 – K	1989	Lincoln Town Car	3"	$2.00
44 – A	1958	Rolls Royce Silver Cloud	2⅝"	$40.00
44 – B	1964	Rolls Royce Phantom V	2⅞"	$35.00
44 – C	1967	GMC Refrigerator Truck with regular wheels	3"	$25.00
44 – D	1970	GMC Refrigerator Truck with SF wheels	3"	$12.00
44 – E	1972	Boss Mustang	2⅞"	$8.00
44 – F	1978	Railway Passenger Coach	3¹⁄₁₆"	$8.00
44 – G	1982	Chevy 4x4 Van	2⅞"	$4.00
44 – H	1983	Citroen 15CV (European model)	3"	$5.00
44 – I	1988	Skoda 130LR Rally (European model)	2⅞"	$4.00
44 – J	1990	1921 Ford Model T Van	2⅞"	$2.00
45 – A	1958	Vauxhall Victor Sedan	2⅜"	$35.00
45 – B	1965	Ford Corsair with boat and rack on roof	2⅝"	$20.00
45 – C	1970	Ford Group 6 with SF wheels only	3"	$15.00
45 – D	1976	BMW 3.0 CSL	2⅞"	$8.00
45 – E	1982	Kenworth COE Aerodyne	2¾"	$3.00
45 – F	1988	Ford Cargo Skip Truck (see 70 – G)	2¹³⁄₁₆"	$2.00
45 – G	1990	Chevrolet Highway Maintenance Truck (see 69 – I)	3"	$2.00

MODEL NUMBER	YEAR INTRODUCED	DESCRIPTION	LENGTH	CURRENT VALUE
46 – A	1958	Morris Minor 1000	2"	$45.00
46 – B	1960	Pickford Removal Van	2⅝"	$60.00
46 – C	1968	Mercedes Benz 300SE with regular wheels	2⅞"	$25.00
46 – D	1970	Mercedes Benz 300SE with SF wheels	2⅞"	$10.00
46 – E	1972	Stretcha Fetcha	2¾"	$6.00
46 – F	1978	Ford Tractor	2³⁄₁₆"	$4.00
46 – G	1982	Hot Chocolate Volkswagen Beetle	2¹³⁄₁₆"	$10.00
46 – H	1983	Big Blue Volkswagen Beetle	2¹³⁄₁₆"	$8.00
46 – I	1985	Mission Chopper with retractable tail	3"	$4.00
46 – J	1985	Sauber Group C Racer	3"	$3.00
47 – A	1958	Trojan 1 Ton Van "BROOKE BOND TEA"	2¼"	$40.00
47 – Ba	1963	Commer Ice Cream Canteen (cream)	2⁷⁄₁₆"	$40.00
47 – Bb	1963	Commer Ice Cream Canteen (blue)	2⁷⁄₁₆"	$30.00
47 – C	1968	DAF Tipper Container Truck with regular wheels	3"	$20.00
47 – D	1970	DAF Tipper Container Truck with SF wheels	3"	$10.00
47 – E	1974	Beach Hopper (Rolamatic)	2⅝"	$6.00
47 – F	1979	Pannier Tank Locomotive	3"	$4.00
47 – G	1982	Jaguar SS100	3"	$3.00
47 – H	1985	School Bus	3"	$2.00
48 – A	1958	Meteor Sports Boat and Trailer (metal)	2⅜"	$35.00
48 – B	1961	Sports Boat and Trailer (plastic boat)	2⅝"	$25.00
48 – C	1966	Dodge Dump Truck with regular wheels	3"	$20.00
48 – D	1970	Dodge Dump Truck with SF wheels	3"	$10.00
48 – E	1972	Pi-Eyed Piper (compare to 48 – G)	2⅞"	$6.00
48 – F	1977	Sambron Jack Lift	3¹⁄₁₆"	$8.00
48 – G	1982	Red Rider (variation of 48 – E)	2⅞"	$3.00
48 – H	1984	Unimog with snowplow	3"	$3.00
48 – I	1987	Vauxhall Astra GTE (European model)	2¾"	$6.00
48 – J	1993	Firebird SE	3"	$2.00
49 – A	1958	Army Halftrack Mk III Personnel Carrier	2½"	$30.00
49 – B	1967	Mercedes Unimog with regular wheels	2½"	$20.00
49 – C	1970	Mercedes Unimog with SF wheels	2½"	$15.00

MODEL NUMBER	YEAR INTRODUCED	DESCRIPTION	LENGTH	CURRENT VALUE
49 – D	1973	Chop Suey Motorcycle	2¾"	$6.00
49 – E	1976	Crane Truck	2¹⁵/₁₆"	$4.00
49 – F	1983	Sand Digger Volkswagen Beetle	2¹³/₁₆"	$8.00
49 – G	1984	Dune Man Volkswagen Beetle	2¹³/₁₆"	$6.00
49 – H	1987	Peugeot Quasar	2¾"	$2.00
49 – I	1992	Lamborghini Diablo	3"	$2.00
49 – J	1993	BMW 850i	3"	$2.00
50 – A	1958	Commer Pickup Truck	2½"	$50.00
50 – B	1964	John Deere Tractor	2⅛"	$30.00
50 – C	1969	Ford Kennel Truck with four dogs and regular wheels	2¾"	$20.00
50 – D	1970	Ford Kennel Truck with four dogs and SF wheels	2¾"	$12.00
50 – E	1973	Articulated Truck with removable trailer	3¹/₁₆"	$8.00
50 – F	1980	Articulated Trailer	3"	$8.00
50 – G	1980	Harley Davidson Motorcycle	2¹¹/₁₆"	$6.00
50 – H	1985	Chevy Blazer 4x4 Police	3"	$3.00
50 – I	1989	Dodge Dakota Pickup Truck (see 17 – J)	3"	$2.00
50 – J	1991	Mack Auxiliary Power Truck (see 57 – I)	3"	$2.00
51 – A	1958	Albion Chieftain "PORTLAND CEMENT" Truck	2½"	$45.00
51 – B	1964	John Deere Trailer with three barrels	2⅝"	$30.00
51 – C	1969	AEC Ergomatic 8-Wheel Tipper with regular wheels	3"	$15.00
51 – D	1970	AEC Ergomatic 8-Wheel Tipper with SF wheels	3"	$10.00
51 – E	1972	Citroen SM	3"	$8.00
51 – F	1978	Combine Harvester	2¾"	$10.00
51 – G	1982	Midnight Magic (variation of 53 – E)	3"	$6.00
51 – H	1984	Leyland Titan London Bus (see 17 – F)	3"	$5.00
51 – I	1984	Firebird S/E	3"	$2.00
51 – J	1985	Camaro IROC Z	3"	$2.00
51 – K	1988	Ford LTD Police	3"	$2.00
52 – Aa	1958	Maserati 4CL T/1948 with regular wheels	2⅜"	$40.00
52 – Ab	1958	Maserati 4CL T/1948 with spoked wheels	2⅜"	$45.00
52 – B	1965	BRM Racing Car with tires on plastic hubs	2⅝"	$20.00
52 – C	1970	Dodge Charger Mk III (SF only)	2⅞"	$12.00
52 – D	1976	Police Launch	3"	$6.00

MODEL NUMBER	YEAR INTRODUCED	DESCRIPTION	LENGTH	CURRENT VALUE
52 – E	1981	BMW M1 with opening hood; LESNEY	3"	$6.00
52 – Fa	1982	BMW M1 with unopening hood; LESNEY	3"	$4.00
52 – Fb	1983	BMW M1 with unopening hood; MATCHBOX INTL LTD	3"	$2.00
52 – G	1991	Isuzu Amigo	2⁷⁄₈"	$2.00
53 – A	1959	Aston Martin DB2 Saloon	2¹⁵⁄₁₆"	$45.00
53 – B	1963	Mercedes Benz 220SE	2¾"	$40.00
53 – C	1968	Ford Zodiac Mk IV Sedan with regular wheels	2¾"	$25.00
53 – D	1970	Ford Zodiac Mk IV Sedan with SF wheels	2¾"	$8.00
53 – E	1972	Tanzara	3"	$6.00
53 – F	1977	Jeep CJ6	2¹⁵⁄₁₆"	$4.00
53 – Ga	1982	Flareside Pickup	2⁷⁄₈"	$4.00
53 – Gb	1983	Flareside Pickup Baja Bouncer	2⁷⁄₈"	$3.00
53 – H	1989	Faun Dump Truck (see 58 – F)	2¾"	$2.00
53 – I	1992	Ford LTD Taxi	3"	$2.00
54 – A	1959	Army Saracen Personnel Carrier	2¼"	$45.00
54 – B	1965	Cadillac S&S Ambulance with regular wheels	2⁵⁄₈"	$30.00
54 – C	1970	Cadillac S&S Ambulance with SF wheels	2⁷⁄₈"	$12.00
54 – D	1971	Ford Capri	3"	$8.00
54 – E	1976	Personnel Carrier	3"	$4.00
54 – F	1980	Motor Home	3¼"	$12.00
54 – G	1982	NASA Tracking Vehicle (variation of 54 – F)	3¼"	$4.00
54 – H	1985	Airport Foam Pumper (variation of 54 – F)	3¼"	$2.00
54 – I	1990	Chevrolet Lumina Stock Car	3"	$3.00
55 – A	1959	DUKW Army Amphibian	2¾"	$50.00
55 – B	1963	Ford Fairlane Police Car	2⁵⁄₈"	$40.00
55 – C	1966	Ford Galaxie Police Car	2⁷⁄₈"	$30.00
55 – D	1968	Mercury Police Car with regular wheels	3"	$25.00
55 – E	1970	Mercury Police Car with SF wheels	3"	$12.00
55 – F	1971	Mercury Commuter Police Station Wagon	3"	$10.00
55 – G	1975	Hellraiser	3"	$6.00
55 – H	1979	Ford Cortina 1600 GL (green or red)	3¹⁄₁₆"	$4.00
55 – I	1982	Ford Cortina 1600 GL (metallic tan)	3¹⁄₁₆"	$2.00
55 – J	1983	Super Porsche 935 Racer	3"	$2.00

MODEL NUMBER	YEAR INTRODUCED	DESCRIPTION	LENGTH	CURRENT VALUE
55 – K	1983	Ford Sierra XR4i (also see 40 – I, 15 – H, 15 – I)	3"	$2.00
55 – L	1986	Mercury Halley's Comet Commemorative Car (SF – 1 – B)	3"	$4.00
55 – M	1988	Mercury Sable Wagon	3"	$2.00
55 – N	1990	Rolls Royce Silver Spirit	3"	$2.00
55 – O	1993	Model A Hot Rod (prev. 73 – H)	3"	$2.00
56 – A	1959	London Trolley Bus	2⅝"	$60.00
56 – B	1965	Fiat 1500 with luggage on roof	2½"	$25.00
56 – C	1970	BMC 1800 Pininfarina (SF only)	2¾"	$10.00
56 – D	1974	High-Tailer Team Matchbox Racer	3"	$5.00
56 – E	1979	Mercedes 450SEL	3"	$12.00
56 – F	1980	Mercedes 450SEL Taxi	3"	$4.00
56 – G	1982	Peterbilt Tanker (also 5 – I)	3"	$4.00
56 – H	1986	Volkswagen Golf GTi	2⅞"	$2.00
56 – I	1992	Ford LTD Taxi	3"	$2.00
57 – A	1959	Wolseley 1500 Sedan	2⅛"	$45.00
57 – B	1961	Chevrolet Impala	2¾"	$35.00
57 – C	1966	Land Rover Fire Truck with regular wheels	2⅞"	$30.00
57 – D	1970	Land Rover Fire Truck with SF wheels	2⅞"	$10.00
57 – E	1970	Eccles Caravan Travel Trailer	3"	$8.00
57 – F	1973	Wildlife Truck (Rolamatic)	2¾"	$10.00
57 – G	1982	Carmichael Commando (European model)	3"	$14.00
57 – Ha	1982	4x4 Mini Pickup	2¾"	$6.00
57 – Hb	1982	Mountain Man 4x4 Mini Pickup	2¾"	$6.00
57 – I	1985	Mission Chopper (see 46 – I)	3"	$3.00
57 – J	1990	Ford Transit Van	3"	$2.00
57 – K	1991	Mack Floodlight Heavy Rescue Auxiliary Power Truck	3"	$2.00
58 – A	1959	BRITISH EUROPEAN AIRWAYS Coach	2½"	$45.00
58 – B	1962	Drott Excavator	2⅝"	$30.00
58 – C	1968	DAF Girder Truck with regular wheels	2⅝"	$18.00
58 – D	1970	DAF Girder Truck with SF wheels	2⅝"	$8.00
58 – E	1972	Woosh-N-Push	2⅞"	$5.00
58 – F	1976	Faun Dump Truck (see 53 – H)	3"	$4.00
58 – G	1983	Ruff Trek Holden Pickup	2⅞"	$6.00
58 – H	1987	Mercedes Benz 300E	3"	$2.00
58 – I	1982	Corvette T-Top (also 40 – F, 62 – G)	3"	$2.00

MODEL NUMBER	YEAR INTRODUCED	DESCRIPTION	LENGTH	CURRENT VALUE
59 – A	1959	Ford Thames Van "SINGER"	2⅛"	$40.00
59 – B	1963	Ford Fairlane Fire Chief Car	2⅞"	$35.00
59 – C	1966	Ford Galaxie Fire Chief Car with regular wheels	2⅞"	$20.00
59 – D	1970	Ford Galaxie Fire Chief Car with SF wheels	2⅞"	$12.00
59 – E	1971	Mercury Parklane Fire Chief Car	3"	$8.00
59 – F	1975	Planet Scout	2¾"	$6.00
59 – G	1980	Porsche 928	3"	$3.00
59 – H	1988	T-Bird Turbo Coupe (see 61 – F)	3"	$2.00
59 – I	1991	Porsche 944	3"	$2.00
60 – A	1959	Morris J2 Pickup "BUILDERS SUPPLY"	2¼"	$50.00
60 – B	1966	Leyland Site Office Truck with regular wheels	2½"	$25.00
60 – C	1970	Leyland Site Office Truck with SF wheels	2½"	$15.00
60 – D	1971	Lotus Super Seven	3"	$6.00
60 – Ea	1982	Mustang Piston Popper (Rolamatic)	2¹³⁄₁₆"	$3.00
60 – Eb	1983	Mustang "GOOD VIBRATIONS – SUNKIST" Piston Popper	3"	$4.00
60 – F	1984	Pontiac Firebird S/E	3"	$2.00
60 – G	1984	Toyota Celica Supra	3"	$2.00
60 – H	1987	New Ford Transit	2⅞"	$2.00
60 – I	1990	NASA Rocket Transporter	3"	$2.00
61 – A	1959	Ferret Scout Car	2¼"	$35.00
61 – B	1966	Alvis Stalwart "BP EXPLORATION"	2⅝"	$25.00
61 – C	1971	Blue Shark	3"	$8.00
61 – D	1978	Ford Wreck Truck	3"	$6.00
61 – E	1982	Peterbilt Wreck Truck	3"	$4.00
61 – F	1988	Ford T-Bird Turbo Coupe (see 59 – H)	3"	$2.00
61 – G	1990	Nissan 300ZX	3"	$2.00
61 – H	1992	Fork Lift Truck	3⅛"	$2.00
62 – A	1959	General Service Lorry	2⅝"	$35.00
62 – B	1963	TV Service Van with ladder, antenna, and three TV's	2½"	$45.00
62 – C	1968	Mercury Cougar with chrome hubs and doors that open	3"	$20.00
62 – D	1970	Mercury Cougar with SF wheels and doors that open	3"	$8.00
62 – E	1970	Mercury Cougar Rat Rod with unopening doors	3"	$6.00

MODEL NUMBER	YEAR INTRODUCED	DESCRIPTION	LENGTH	CURRENT VALUE
62 – F	1974	Renault 17TL	3"	$10.00
62 – G	1980	Corvette T-Roof	3¹⁄₁₆"	$5.00
62 – H	1983	Corvette Hardtop	3¹⁄₁₆"	$4.00
62 – I	1985	Rolls Royce Silver Cloud	3"	$2.00
62 – J	1985	Volvo Container Truck	3¹⁄₁₆"	$2.00
62 – K	1987	Volvo 760 (European model)	3"	$4.00
62 – L	1989	Oldsmobile Aerotech	3"	$2.00
63 – A	1959	Ford 3-Ton Service Ambulance	2½"	$35.00
63 – B	1964	Airport Crash Tender	2¼"	$35.00
63 – C	1968	Dodge Crane Truck with regular wheels	2¾"	$20.00
63 – D	1970	Dodge Crane Truck with SF wheels	2¾"	$10.00
63 – E	1973	Freeway Gas Tanker	3"	$6.00
63 – F	1978	Freeway Gas Tanker Trailer	3"	$6.00
63 – G	1980	Dodge Challenger/Mitsubishi Galant Eterna	2⅞"	$6.00
63 – H	1982	Snorkel Fire Engine with open cab	2¹³⁄₁₆"	$3.00
63 – I	1984	4x4 Pickup	3"	$2.00
64 – A	1959	Scammell Breakdown Truck	2½"	$35.00
64 – B	1966	MG 1100 with driver and dog; regular wheels	2⅝"	$20.00
64 – C	1970	MG 1100 with driver and dog; SF wheels	2⅝"	$10.00
64 – D	1971	Slingshot Dragster	3"	$6.00
64 – E	1976	Fire Chief	3"	$4.00
64 – F	1979	Caterpillar Bulldozer with plastic roof	2⅝"	$4.00
64 – G	1985	Dodge Caravan	3"	$3.00
64 – H	1990	Oldsmobile Aerotech	3"	$2.00
65 – A	1959	3.4 Litre Jaguar	2½"	$35.00
65 – B	1962	3.8 Litre Jaguar	2⅝"	$30.00
65 – C	1967	Claas Combine Harvester (regular wheels only)	3"	$15.00
65 – D	1973	Saab Sonnet (SF wheels only)	2¾"	$6.00
65 – Ea	1977	Airport Coach "AMERICAN AIRWAYS"	3"	$10.00
65 – Eb	1977	Airport Coach "BRITISH AIRWAYS"	3"	$10.00
65 – Ec	1977	Airport Coach "LUFTHANSA"	3"	$10.00
65 – Ed	1977	Airport Coach "QUANTAS"	3"	$12.00
65 – Ee	1977	Airport Coach "SCHULBUS"	3"	$15.00

MODEL NUMBER	YEAR INTRODUCED	DESCRIPTION	LENGTH	CURRENT VALUE
65 – F	1982	Tyrone Malone Bandag Bandit	3"	$2.00
65 – G	1984	Indy Racer	3"	$2.00
65 – H	1986	Plane Transporter "RESCUE"	3"	$2.00
65 – I	1988	Cadillac Allante	3"	$2.00
66 – A	1959	Citroen DS19	2½"	$45.00
66 – B	1962	Harley Davidson Motorcycle and Sidecar	2⅝"	$50.00
66 – Ca	1967	Greyhound Bus with regular wheels and clear windows	3"	$30.00
66 – Cb	1968	Greyhound Bus with regular wheels and amber windows	3"	$25.00
66 – D	1970	Greyhound Bus with SF wheels	3"	$20.00
66 – E	1971	Mazda RX500	3"	$15.00
66 – F	1977	Ford Transit	2¾"	$8.00
66 – G	1982	Tyrone Malone Super Boss	3"	$4.00
66 – H	1985	Sauber Group C Racer	3"	$3.00
66 – I	1988	Rolls Royce Silver Spirit	3"	$2.00
67 – A	1959	Saladin Armoured Car	2½"	$40.00
67 – B	1967	Volkswagen 1600TL with chrome hubs	2¾"	$25.00
67 – C	1970	Volkswagen 1600TL with SF wheels	2¾"	$15.00
67 – D	1973	Hot Rocker Mercury Capri	3"	$12.00
67 – E	1978	Datsun 260Z 2+2	3"	$8.00
67 – F	1983	Flame Out (variation of 48 – E and 48 – G)	3"	$6.00
67 – G	1983	IMSA Mustang (see 11 – I)	3"	$4.00
67 – H	1985	Lamborghini Countach LP500S	3"	$2.00
67 – I	1987	Icarus Bus (European model)	3"	$5.00
68 – A	1959	Austin Mk 2 Radio Truck	2⅜"	$45.00
68 – Ba	1965	Mercedes Coach with orange lower body	2⅞"	$30.00
68 – Bb	1965	Mercedes Coach with sea green lower body	2⅞"	$120.00
68 – C	1970	Porsche 910 (SF wheels only)	2⅞"	$12.00
68 – D	1975	Cosmobile	2⅞"	$8.00
68 – E	1979	Chevy Van	2¹⁵⁄₁₆"	$5.00
68 – F	1984	Dodge Caravan (see 64 – G)	2⅞"	$2.00
68 – G	1987	Camaro IROC Z	3"	$2.00
68 – H	1989	TV News Truck	3"	$2.00
68 – I	1992	Road Roller	3"	$2.00

MODEL NUMBER	YEAR INTRODUCED	DESCRIPTION	LENGTH	CURRENT VALUE
69 – A	1959	Commer 30CWT Van "NESTLE'S"	2¼"	$50.00
69 – B	1965	Hatra Tractor Shovel	3"	$65.00
69 – C	1969	Rolls Royce Silver Shadow Convertible (SF wheels only)	3"	$15.00
69 – D	1973	Turbo Fury	3"	$8.00
69 – E	1978	Armored Truck "WELLS FARGO"	2¹³⁄₁₆"	$8.00
69 – F	1982	1933 Willys Street Rod	2¹⁵⁄₁₆"	$4.00
69 – G	1983	1983 Corvette	3"	$2.00
69 – H	1989	Volvo 480ES (European model)	2⅞"	$5.00
69 – I	1990	Chevrolet Highway Maintenance Truck	3¹⁄₁₆"	$2.00
70 – A	1959	Ford Thames Estate Car	2⅛"	$40.00
70 – B	1966	Atkinson Grit Spreader with regular wheels	2⅝"	$30.00
70 – C	1970	Atkinson Grit Spreader with SF wheels	2⅝"	$15.00
70 – D	1971	Dodge Dragster	3"	$6.00
70 – E	1976	Self-Propelled Gun	2⅝"	$8.00
70 – F	1981	Ferrari 308 GTB	2¹⁵⁄₁₆"	$4.00
70 – G	1988	Ford Skip Truck	2¹³⁄₁₆"	$2.00
70 – H	1989	Ferrari F40	3"	$2.00
70 – I	1993	Military Tank	2⅞"	$2.00
71 – A	1959	Austin 200-Gallon Water Truck	2⅜"	$35.00
71 – B	1964	Jeep Gladiator Pickup Truck	2⅝"	$25.00
71 – C	1968	Ford Heavy Wreck Truck "ESSO" with regular wheels	3"	$20.00
71 – D	1970	Ford Heavy Wreck Truck "ESSO" with SF wheels	3"	$10.00
71 – E	1973	Jumbo Jet Motorcycle	2¾"	$6.00
71 – F	1976	Dodge Cattle Truck with cattle (see 4 – E)	3"	$4.00
71 – G	1982	1962 Corvette	2¹⁵⁄₁₆"	$2.00
71 – H	1986	Scania T142	3"	$2.00
71 – I	1988	Porsche 944 Racer	3"	$2.00
71 – J	1989	GMC Wrecker	3"	$2.00
72 – A	1959	Fordson Power Major Farm Tractor	2"	$40.00
72 – B	1966	Standard Jeep CJ5 with plastic wheel hubs	2⅜"	$20.00
72 – C	1970	Standard Jeep CJ5 with SF wheels	2⅜"	$10.00
72 – D	1972	Hovercraft SRN6	3"	$15.00

MODEL NUMBER	YEAR INTRODUCED	DESCRIPTION	LENGTH	CURRENT VALUE
72 – E	1973	Maxi Taxi Mercury Capri	3"	$6.00
72 – F	1979	Bomag Road Roller	2¹⁵⁄₁₆"	$4.00
72 – G	1982	Dodge Delivery Truck (European model)	2¾"	$8.00
72 – H	1984	Sand Racer	2¹¹⁄₁₆"	$2.00
72 – I	1985	Plane Transporter "RESCUE"	3"	$2.00
72 – J	1986	Scania T142	3"	$2.00
72 – K	1987	Ford Superman II	3"	$2.00
72 – L	1988	Cadillac Allante	3"	$2.00
72 – M	1989	GMC Wrecker	3"	$2.00
73 – A	1959	RAF 10-Ton Pressure Refueling Tanker	2⅝"	$40.00
73 – B	1962	Ferrari F1 Racing Car	2⅝"	$45.00
73 – C	1968	Mercury Commuter Station Wagon with chrome hubs	3⅛"	$15.00
73 – D	1970	Mercury Commuter Station Wagon with SF wheels	3"	$8.00
73 – E	1972	Mercury Commuter with raised roof	3"	$15.00
73 – F	1974	Weasel Armored Vehicle	2⅞"	$8.00
73 – G	1979	Model "A" Ford with spare tire cast into fender	2¹³⁄₁₆"	$12.00
73 – H	1980	Model "A" Ford with no spare tire cast into fender	2¹³⁄₁₆"	$6.00
73 – I	1990	Mercedes 1600 Turbo Farm Tractor	3"	$2.00
73 – J	1990	TV News Truck	3"	$2.00
74 – A	1959	Mobile Canteen Refreshment Bar	2⅝"	$60.00
74 – B	1966	Daimler London Bus with regular wheels	3"	$30.00
74 – C	1970	Daimler London Bus with SF wheels	3"	$15.00
74 – D	1972	Toe Joe Wreck Truck	2¾"	$8.00
74 – E	1978	Cougar Villager Station Wagon	3"	$6.00
74 – F	1981	Orange Peel Dodge Charger	3"	$4.00
74 – G	1984	Fiat Abarth	3"	$2.00
74 – H	1987	Toyota MR2	2⅞"	$2.00
74 – I	1987	Ford Utility Truck	3"	$2.00
74 – J	1988	Williams Honda F1 Grand Prix Racer	3"	$2.00
75 – A	1960	Ford Thunderbird	2⅝"	$45.00
75 – Ba	1965	Ferrari Berlinetta with spoked wheel hubs	3"	$40.00
75 – Bb	1965	Ferrari Berlinetta with chrome wheel hubs	3"	$35.00
75 – C	1970	Ferrari Berlinetta with SF wheels	3"	$12.00

MODEL NUMBER	YEAR INTRODUCED	DESCRIPTION	LENGTH	CURRENT VALUE
75 – D	1971	Alfa Carabo	3"	$10.00
75 – E	1977	Seasprite Helicopter with small windows	2¾"	$8.00
75 – F	1982	Helicopter with pilot and large windows	3"	$4.00
75 – G	1987	Ferrari Testarossa	3"	$2.00

40TH ANNIVERSARY COLLECTION & MATCHBOX ORIGINALS

In 1988 Matchbox produced a set of five models celebrating the 40th anniversary (1947 – 1987) of Lesney Products. Replicas of 1 – A Diesel Road Roller, 4 – A Massey Harris Tractor, 5 – A London Bus, 7 – A Horse Drawn Milk Cart, and 9 – A Dennis Fire Escape are included in a yellow matchbox-style package. The models are authentic replicas of the originals with minor exceptions.

In 1991 Matchbox repackaged these replicas individually in a blister pack which includes an authentic box and marketed them as "MATCHBOX ORIGINALS." Color and marking variations differentiate them from the 40th Anniversary Collection mentioned above.

In 1993 Matchbox Originals Series II was introduced to continue the line of reproductions of early models. Although these models are listed under the appropriate model number and introduction year, the major variations are listed below for ease of recognition.

MODEL NUMBER	YEAR INTRODUCED	DESCRIPTION	CURRENT VALUE
DIESEL ROAD ROLLER		1⅞"	
1 – A	1953	Green body with no model number imprinted	$55.00
1 – La	1988	Green body, "MATCHBOX MADE IN CHINA" under roof, "1988" on bottom inside of body	$10.00
1 – Lb	1991	Blue body, "MATCHBOX MADE IN CHINA" under roof, "1988" on bottom inside of body	$3.00
MASSEY HARRIS TRACTOR		1⅝"	
4 – A	1954	Red with gray metal tires, "LESNEY ENGLAND" on sides of fenders	$65.00
4 – Ja	1988	Red with silver metal tires, "MATCHBOX MADE IN CHINA" on sides of fenders	$10.00
4 – Jb	1991	Green with silver metal tires, "MATCHBOX MADE IN CHINA" on sides of fenders	$3.00
LONDON BUS		2"	
5 – A	1954	Red with gray metal wheels, "BUY 'MATCHBOX' SERIES"	$60.00
5 – Ja	1988	Red with silver metal wheels, "BUY 'MATCHBOX' SERIES," "MATCHBOX MADE IN CHINA 1988" on bottom	$10.00
5 – Jb	1991	Red with silver metal wheels, "MATCHBOX ORIGINALS" "MATCHBOX MADE IN CHINA" on bottom	$3.00
QUARRY TRUCK		2⅛"	
6 – Aa	1954	Orange with gray dumper and metal wheels	$55.00
6 – Ab	1954	Orange with gray dumper and plastic wheels	$50.00
6 – K	1993	Blue with gray dumper	$3.00
QUARRY TRUCK		2¼"	
7 – A	1954	Orange with gray metal wheels, "MATCHBOX MADE IN CHINA 1988" on bottom, harness is diecast to base	$90.00

MODEL NUMBER	YEAR INTRODUCED	DESCRIPTION	CURRENT VALUE
7 – Ka	1988	Orange with silver metal wheels, "MATCHBOX MADE IN CHINA 1988" on bottom, harness is riveted to base	$10.00
7 – Kb	1991	Light blue with silver metal wheels, "MATCHBOX MADE IN CHINA 1988" on bottom, harness is riveted to base	$3.00
DENNIS FIRE ESCAPE		2¼"	
9 – A	1955	No number cast in body, red reels on back with gray metal wheels	$60.00
9 – Ia	1988	"MATCHBOX MADE IN CHINA 1988" on base, red reels on back with silver metal wheels	$10.00
9 – Ib	1991	"MATCHBOX MADE IN CHINA 1988" on base, yellow reels on back with silver metal wheels	$3.00
BEDFORD WRECK TRUCK		2"	
13 – A	1955	Tan body with red boom	$45.00
13 – J	1993	Red body with yellow boom	$3.00
MG MIDGET SPORTS CAR		2"	
19 – A	1956	Cream or white body with metal wheels	$50.00
19 – I	1993	Green body with plastic wheels	$3.00
FODEN READY MIX CONCRETE TRUCK		1¾"	
26 – A	1956	Orange body, gray barrel, "Lesney England" on base	$65.00
26 – K	1993	Orange body, gray barrel, "MATCHBOX" on base	$3.00
JAGUAR XK140 COUPE		2⅜"	
32 – A	1957	Cream or red body	$50.00
32 – I	1993	Black body	$3.00

GIFT SETS & PROMOTIONAL ITEMS

Hundreds of gift sets, playsets and promotional items have been produced since the beginning. Too numerous to list, they are nevertheless significant to the collector to examine briefly.

The 1966 Collector Catalog illustrates sets available from Matchbox at the time, and includes retail prices for the items.

The GS – 1 Service Station Set for example originally sold for $5.50 and included MG – 1 Service Station, originally $3.00, A – 1 Accessory Pack — Garage Pumps and Forecourt Sign, for 65¢ separately, and regular series models number 13 Dodge Wreck Truck, number 31 Lincoln Continental, and number 64 MG 1100, for 55¢ each. The current (1992) value of this set in original container is $80.00 – 120.00. This is just an example. An entire book could be devoted just to gift sets, games, playsets, dolls, toys and promotional items manufactured under the Matchbox name.

THE NEW SUPERFAST

In 1986 Matchbox reintroduced the SuperFast series as a 24-model collection derived from the 1–75 series. These models are distinguished by wide tires, each with a raised chrome-colored twelve-pointed star inside a large chrome circle whose diameter is almost that of the tire itself. Some models have different markings and colors than their regular series counterpart (as indicated in parentheses), but others are identical except for the distinctive wheels. No new models have been added since 1988.

MODEL NUMBER	DESCRIPTION	LENGTH	CURRENT VALUE
SF – 1 – Aa	Mercury Parklane Police Car (55 – E,1970; 55 – L, 1986)	3"	$2.00
SF – 1 – Ab	Mercury Parklane Halley's Comet Commemorative Car	3"	$5.00
SF – 2 – Aa	1982 Firebird S/E (12 – I, 1982)	3"	$2.00
SF – 2 – Ab	1982 Firebird S/E Halley's Comet Commemorative Car	3"	$5.00
SF – 3 – A	Porsche 928 (59 – G, 1980)	3"	$2.00
SF – 4 – A	1984 Dodge Daytona Turbo Z (28 – I, 1984)	2⁷⁄₈"	$2.00
SF – 5 – A	AMG Mercedes Benz 500SEC (43 – I, 1984)	2⁷⁄₈"	$2.00
SF – 6 – A	Porsche 935 (55 – J, 1983)	3"	$2.00
SF – 7 – A	Ford Sierra XR4Ti (15 – H/15 – I/40 – I/55 – K, 1983)	3"	$2.00
SF – 8 – A	1962 Corvette (71 – G, 1982)	2¹⁵⁄₁₆"	$2.00
SF – 9 – A	Datsun 280ZX Turbo 2+2 (24 – H, 1982)	3"	$2.00
SF – 10 – A	Buick LeSabre (10 – H, 1987)	3"	$2.00
SF – 11 – A	Ferrari 308GTB (70 – F, 1981)	2¹⁵⁄₁₆"	$2.00
SF – 12 – Aa	Chevy Pro Stocker (34 – G/34 – I, 1981)	3"	$3.00
SF – 12 – Ab	Chevy Pro Stocker Halley's Comet Commemorative Car	3"	$5.00
SF – 12 – B	Cadillac Allante (72 – I/65 – G, 1988)	3"	$2.00
SF – 13 – A	1984 Corvette (14 – J, 1984)	3"	$2.00
SF – 14 – A	BMW 323i Cabriolet (39 – G, 1985)	2¾"	$2.00
SF – 15 – A	Ford Escort XR3i Cabriolet (17 – I, 1985)	2¾"	$2.00
SF – 16 – A	Sauber Group C Racer (66 – G, 1985)	3"	$2.00
SF – 17 – A	Lamborghini Countach LP500S (67 – G, 1985)	3"	$2.00
SF – 18 – A	Firebird Racer (60 – F, 1984)	3"	$2.00
SF – 19 – A	Pontiac Fiero Racer (2 – I, 1985)	2¹³⁄₁₆"	$2.00
SF – 20	Not Issued		Not Issued
SF – 21 – A	Nissan 300ZX Turbo (24 – I, 1987)	2⁷⁄₈"	$2.00
SF – 22 – A	Camaro IROC Z (51 – J, 1985)	3"	$2.00
SF – 23 – A	Toyota MR2 (9 – H, 1987)	2⅝"	$2.00
SF – 24 – A	Ferrari Testarossa (75 – G, 1987)	3"	$2.00
SF – 25 – A	Peugeot Quasar (49 – H, 1987)	2¾"	$2.00

LASER WHEELS

Thirty models make up this line introduced in 1987 with "prism" wheels that refract light into rainbow colors similar to the surface of a laser audio or video disc, hence the name Laser Wheels. Current value on all models in this series is $4.00 to $5.00 each. Each model's regular series counterpart is indicated in parentheses.

MODEL NUMBER	MODEL DESCRIPTION	
1987		
LW – 1 – A	Mercury Police Car (55 – E, 1970)	3"
LW – 2 – A	1982 Firebird (12 – I, 1982)	3"
LW – 3 – A	Porsche 928 (59 – G, 1980)	3"
LW – 4 – A	Dodge Daytona Turbo Z (28 – I, 1984)	2⅞"
LW – 5 – A	AMG Mercedes Benz 500SEC (43 – I, 1984)	2⅞"
LW – 6 – A	Porsche 935 (55 – J, 1985)	3"
LW – 7 – A	Sierra XR4 (15 – H, 15 – I, 40 – I, 55 – N, 1983)	3"
LW – 8 – A	1962 Corvette (71 – G, 1982)	2¹⁵⁄₁₆"
LW – 9 – A	Datsun 280ZX Turbo (24 – H, 1982)	3"
LW – 10 – A	Turbo Corvette (21 – H, 1983)	3"
LW – 11 – A	Ferrari 308GTB (70 – F, 1981)	2¹⁵⁄₁₆"
LW – 12 – A	Chevy Pro Stocker (34 – G, 34 – I, 1981)	3"
LW – 13 – A	1984 Corvette (14 – J, 1984)	3"
LW – 14 – A	BMW 323i Cabriolet (39 – G, 1985)	2¾"
LW – 15 – A	Escort XR3i Cabriolet (17 – I, 1985)	2¾"
LW – 16 – A	Sauber Group C Racer (66 – G, 1985)	3"

MODEL NUMBER	MODEL DESCRIPTION	
LW – 17 – A	Lamborghini Countach LP500S (67 – G, 1985)	3"
LW – 18 – A	Firebird Racer (60 – F, 1984)	3"
LW – 19 – A	Fiero Racer (2 – I, 1985)	2¹³⁄₁₆"
LW – 20 – A	Nissan 300ZX Turbo (24 – I, 1987)	2⅞"
LW – 21 – A	Camaro IROC Z (51 – J, 1985)	3"
LW – 22 – A	Toyota MR2 (9 – H, 1987)	2⅝"
LW – 23 – A	Ferrari Testarossa (75 – G, 1987)	3"
LW – 24 – A	Peugeot Quasar (49 – H, 1987)	2¾"
1988		
LW – 25 – A	Buick LeSabre (10 – H, 1988)	3"
LW – 26 – A	Cadillac Allante (72 – I, 65 – G, 1988)	3"
LW – 27 – A	Saab 9000 Turbo (15 – K, 1988)	3"
LW – 28 – A	Rover Sterling (31 – J, 1988)	2¹⁵⁄₁₆"
LW – 29 – A	T-Bird Turbo Coupe (59 – H, 61 – F, 1988)	3"
LW – 30 – A	Volvo 480ES (69 – H, 1989)	2⅞"

LASERTRONICS

Lasertronics were new models for 1990 that are based on selected models from the regular 1–75 series. The models contain electronic sirens and lights that are activated when the wheels are depressed. Current value on all models in this series is $5.00 to $6.00 each.

Mercedes G-Wagon (based on 30 – H, 1984)   3"
    Variations: SWAT, FIRE , AUTO RESCUE

AMG Mercedes (based on 43 – H, 1984)   3"
    Variations: POLICE, MEDIC, PACE CAR

Ford Supervan (based on 6 – I, 1985)   3"
    Variations: POLICE, FIRE , AMBULANCE

Ford Sierra (based on 15 – H, 1983)   3"
    Variations: SHERIFF, AIRPORT SECURITY, FIRE DEPT.

WORLD CLASS

In 1989, Matchbox introduced eight models from the regular series with opaque mirror windows, distinctive paint jobs and realistic Goodyear rubber tires. Each year, new models or variations have been added to the line. Current value is based on introduction year. Models are typically about 3" long.

1989 SERIES I, $6.00 – 8.00 EACH

    Porsche 928s (dark silver)

    Lamborghini Countach LP500S (yellow)

    AMG 500 SEC Mercedes (white)

    '88 Corvette Convertible Roadster (metallic blue)

    Porsche 944 Turbo (black)

    Ferrari Testarossa (red)

    Ferrari 308 GTB (red)

    Porsche 959 (silver)

1990 SERIES II, $5.00 – 7.00 EACH

    Rolls Royce Silver Cloud (metallic yellow)

    Ferrari F-40 (red)

    Thunderbird Turbo Coupe (silver)

    Cadillac Allante (dark silver)

    BMW M-1 (yellow)

    Lincoln Town Car (black)

    Jaguar XK120 (white)

    Corvette Grand Sport (metallic red)

1991 SERIES III, $4.00 – 6.00 EACH

    '57 Chevy (metallic red)

    Lamborghini Countach LP500S (red)

    Nissan 300ZX (white)

    Mercedes 500SL Convertible (black)

    Porsche 935 (yellow)

    '62 Corvette (light blue with white roof)

    Ferrari Testarossa (white)

    Corvette T-Roof (orange)

1992 EDITION, $3.00 – 5.00 EACH

    Lamborghini Diablo (red)

    Mercedes 500SL (silver)

    Corvette T-Roof (blue)

    Nissan 300ZX (red)

    Porsche 935 (white)

    Ferrari F40 (yellow)

1993 EDITION, $3.00 – 4.00 EACH

    Lamborghini Diablo (black)

    BMW 850i (silver)

    '88 Corvette Convertible Roadster (white)

    Ford F-150 (red)

    Cadillac Allante (red)

    Jaguar XJ220 (metallic purple)

MATCHBOX PRESCHOOL

In 1991 a series of regular series models painted in bright primary colors with colorful markings and packaged in sets for preschoolers was introduced. Although shown in the 1991 dealer catalog with appendages such as a boom on the utility truck, the actual models are conspicuously missing such details that may be removed and accidentally swallowed by small children. The Snorkel Fire Truck is similarly missing its boom, and the Volvo Covered Truck is missing its cargo cover. These models serve as an interesting contrast to the detailing of other models and sets. The Preschool models are generally sold in three car sets, and playsets are available to accompany the sets. The current value for an individual model is $2.00, while each five car set is valued at $10.00. For value comparison, see the regular series counterpart.

SUPER GT, CODE II, & CODE III

What distinguishes Super GT models from the regular series is that these models are generally packaged in budget priced sets of 10, 20, or other multiples, and generally have less impressive paint jobs and detailing.

In the case of Code II models, independent companies are licensed by Matchbox to alter color and markings to produce a special limited edition model commemorating an event, product, company, or organization. Values are often doubled or even tripled on such models.

A third case, Code III's, is that in the late fifties and early sixties Matchbox produced inexpensive models with less detailed dies and coloring, generally with no windows. These models are not identified as being made by Lesney and only say "Made in England" on the base.

In the Sixties, at least two manufacturers produced illegal, unlicensed duplicates of Matchbox toys, even so far as duplicating the name "MATCHBOX" on the package; these models are by most collector standards worthless. Unless the models have "Lesney" on them, the collector shouldn't pay more for them than what they are worth as a curiosity. In the late eighties other companies produced models that looked almost identical to Matchbox models, even with the same style wheels. Distinguishing between the two can be difficult. Debate continues between collectors regarding the value of such models, but most agree they are worth considerably less than the Lesney- and Matchbox-marked models.

M.C. Toys (stands for "May Cheong"), based in Asia, is most noted for duplicating scale and detail on models at such a high level that some confuse these with Matchbox toys. The relative value of these models is nearly comparable to Matchbox models by most collectible standards. A bit of advice to collectors: never underestimate the potential value of any model and always be wary in the marketplace when considering buying, selling, and trading models. A few examples are included in the photo section of this book.

900 SERIES, TWO PACKS, TWIN PACKS, & TRAILER SERIES

Variously listed under one of the headings indicated above, this series is defined by its packaging. Two Packs is usually described as a vehicle accompanied by a trailer; however, some of these models are not available separately. One such trailer available only as part of a set is the Glider Trailer included with TP – 7 – B in 1977, TP – 102 – A in 1984, TP – 118 – A in 1987, and TP – 122 – A in 1989. These sets first appeared in the 1976 catalog, although packages of two complementary models were available as early as 1968 with models such as 1 – E Mercedes Benz Lorry and matching 2 – D Mercedes Trailer. The pair was reintroduced as TP – 1 in 1976 with SuperFast wheels.

Since most models in this series are available separately, values listed below are for mint sets in their original containers (MOC). All models are 6 – 6½" long.

MODEL NUMBER	YEAR INTRODUCED	DESCRIPTION	CURRENT VALUE
TP – 1 – A	1976	Mercedes Truck and Trailer	$15.00
TP – 2 – A	1976	Tractor and Trailer	$10.00
TP – 2 – B	1979	Mercury Police and Merryweather Fire Engine	$7.00

MODEL NUMBER	YEAR INTRODUCED	DESCRIPTION	CURRENT VALUE
TP – 2 – C	1980	Mercury Police and Blaze Buster Fire Engine	$6.00
TP – 3 – A	1976	Javelin and Pony Trailer	$8.00
TP – 4 – A	1976	Holiday Set Ford Capri and Eccles Caravan	$8.00
TP – 4 – B	1979	Holiday Set Pantera and Eccles Caravan	$6.00
TP – 5– A	1976	Weekender Guildsman and Boat Trailer	$10.00
TP – 5 – B	1980	Weekender Capri and Boat Trailer	$8.00
TP – 6 – A	1976	Breakdown Truck and Austin Mini	$12.00
TP – 7 – A	1976	Stretcha Fetcha and Mercury Fire Chief	$12.00
TP – 7 – B	1977	Jeep and Glide Trailer	$10.00
TP – 8 – A	1976	Transport Set London Bus and SRN6 Hovercraft	$10.00
TP – 8 – B	1977	Field Car and Motorcycle Trailer	$8.00
TP – 9 – A	1978	Field Car and Team Matchbox Racer	$6.00
TP – 10 – A	1978	Mercedes Ambulance and Mercury Fire Chief	$12.00
TP – 11 – A	1977	Military Jeep and Motorcycle	$7.00
TP – 11– B	1979	Tractor and Hay Trailer	$6.00
TP – 12 – A	1977	Military Field Car and Volkswagen Van	$8.00
TP – 12 – B	1979	Military Jeep and Volkswagen Van	$7.00
TP – 13 – A	1977	Military Scout and Armored Car	$7.00
TP – 13 – B	1979	Military Unimog and Weasel	$7.00
TP – 14 – A	1977	Mercedes Tanker and Radar Truck	$8.00
TP – 14 – B	1979	Mercedes Staff Car and Ambulance	$6.00
TP – 15 – A	1977	Military Mercedes Truck and Trailer	$8.00
TP – 16 – A	1977	Military Dump Truck and Bulldozer	$8.00
TP – 16 – B	1979	Military Alvis Stalwart and Dodge Wrecker	$7.00
TP – 16 – C	1980	Articulated Truck and Trailer	$10.00
TP – 17 – A	1979	Highway Tanker and Trailer	$10.00
TP – 18 – A	1979	Water Sporter Rabbit, Seafire Boat and Trailer	$6.00
TP – 19 – A	1979	Dodge Cattle Truck and Trailer	$6.00
TP – 20 – A	1979	Diesel Shunter and Side Tipper	$10.00
TP – 21 – A	1979	Citroen and Trailer with three plastic motorcycles	$8.00
TP – 22 – A	1979	Long Haul Double Container Truck (later Convoy model)	$12.00
TP – 23 – A	1979	Long Haul Covered Truck (later Convoy model)	$12.00
TP – 24 – A	1979	Long Haul Box Container Truck (later Convoy model)	$12.00
TP – 25 – A	1979	Long Haul Truck and Pipe Trailer (later Convoy model)	$12.00
TP – 102 – A	1984	Ford Escort and Glider Trailer	$5.00
TP – 103 – A	1984	Cattle Truck and Trailer	$5.00

MODEL NUMBER	YEAR INTRODUCED	DESCRIPTION	CURRENT VALUE
TP – 106 – A	1984	Renault 5TL and Motorcycle Trailer	$5.00
TP – 107 – A	1984	Datsun and Caravan	$6.00
TP – 108 – A	1984	Tractor and Trailer	$5.00
TP – 109 – A	1984	Citroen and Boat "POLICE-MARINE DIVISION"	$6.00
TP – 110 – A	1984	Matra Rancho and Inflatable Boat	$6.00
TP – 111 – A	1984	Ford Cortina and Horse Box	$6.00
TP – 112 – A	1984	Unimog and Trailer	$5.00
TP – 113 – A	1985	Porsche and Caravan	$5.00
TP – 114 – A	1985	VW Golf and Horse Box	$5.00
TP – 115 – A	1987	Ford Escort and Boat Trailer	$4.00
TP – 116 – A	1987	Jeep Cherokee and Caravan	$6.00
TP – 117– A	1987	Mercedes G-Wagon and Horse Box	$4.00
TP – 118 – A	1987	BMW and Glider Trailer	$4.00
TP – 119 – A	1987	Flareside Pickup and Seafire Boat	$4.00
TP – 120 – A	1989	VW Golf and Inflatable Raft	$4.00
TP – 121 – A	1989	Land Rover 90 and Seafire Boat	$5.00
TP – 122 – A	1989	Porsche and Glider Trailer	$4.00
TP – 123 – A	1989	BMW Cabriolet and Caravan	$4.00
TP – 124 – A	1989	Zoo Truck and Trailer Caravan	$4.00
TP – 124 – B	1991	Locomotive and Carriage	$6.00
TP – 125 – A	1991	Shunter and Tipper	$6.00
TP – 126 – A	1991	Mercedes Farm Tractor and Hay Trailer	$5.00
TP – 127 – A	1991	BMW and Inflatable Raft	$4.00
TP – 128 – A	1992	Volvo Covered Truck and Trailer	$4.00
TP – 129 – A	1992	Isuzu Amigo and Powerboat	$4.00

CONVOY AND HIGHWAY EXPRESS SERIES (SUPER RIGS, 1993)

1982 saw the introduction of the new Convoy series, derived from the semi tractor/trailers from the Twin Pack Series of the previous year. The Convoy series designation was changed to HE for Highway Express in 1983 and changed back to Convoy the following year. When Tyco purchased Matchbox in 1992, they changed the name again to Super Rigs. All models are approximatley 7½" long.

MODEL NUMBER	YEAR INTRODUCED	DESCRIPTION	CURRENT VALUE
CY – 1 – A	1982	Kenworth Car Transporter (HE – 1 in 1983)	$12.00
CY – 2 – A	1982	Kenworth Rocket Transporter (HE – 2 in 1983)	$8.00
CY – 3 – A	1982	Kenworth Double Container Truck (HE – 3, TP – 22)	$12.00
CY – 4 – A	1982	Kenworth Boat Transporter (HE – 2 in 1983)	$10.00
CY – 5 – A	1982	Peterbilt Covered Truck (HE – 5, TP – 23)	$12.00
CY – 6 – A	1982	Kenworth Horse Box Transporter (HE – 6 in 1983)	$10.00
CY – 7 – A	1982	Peterbilt Petrol Tanker (HE – 7 in 1983)	$8.00
CY – 8 – A	1982	Kenworth C.O.E. Box Truck (HE – 8 in 1983)	$8.00
CY – 9 – A	1982	Kenworth Conventional Box Truck (HE – 9, TP – 24)	$10.00
HE – 10 – A	1983	Kenworth C.O.E. Racing Car Transporter (CY – 10)	$8.00
HE – 11 – A	1983	Kenworth C.O.E. Helicopter Transporter (CY – 11)	$8.00
CY – 12 – B	1984	Kenworth Aircraft Transporter	$6.00
CY – 13 – A	1984	Peterbilt Fire Engine	$6.00
CY – 14 – B	1985	Kenworth C.O.E. Power Launch Transporter	$6.00
CY – 15 – A	1985	Peterbilt NASA Tracking Vehicle	$6.00
CY – 15 – B	1989	Peterbilt "MBTV NEWS" Remote Truck	$5.00
CY – 16 – A	1985	Scania Box Truck	$6.00
CY – 17 – A	1985	Scania Petrol Tanker	$6.00
CY – 18 – A	1986	Scania Container Truck	$6.00
CY – 19 – A	1987	Peterbilt Box Car	$5.00
CY – 20 – A	1987	Kenworth C.O.E. Tipper	$5.00
CY – 21 – A	1987	DAF Aircraft Transporter	$5.00
CY – 22 – C	1987	DAF Power Launch Transporter	$5.00
CY – 23 – A	1988	Scania Covered Truck	$5.00
CY – 24 – Aa	1988	DAF Box Car "PORSCHE"	$5.00
CY – 24 – Ab	1988	DAF Box Car "FERRARI"	$5.00
CY – 25 – A	1988	DAF Box Truck	$5.00
CY – 27 – A	1989	Mack Box Truck	$5.00

MODEL NUMBER	YEAR INTRODUCED	DESCRIPTION	CURRENT VALUE
CY – 28 – A	1989	Mack Container Truck	$5.00
CY – 29 – A	1991	Mack Aircraft Transporter	$5.00
CY – 35 – A	1992	Mack Tanker	$5.00

In 1993, Convoy models are marketed and packaged as Super Rigs. Variations on existing models continue to add value to the collection.

TEAM CONVOY, TEAM MATCHBOX & CONVOY ACTION PACKS

Team Convoy and Convoy Action Packs consist of Convoy Models and accompanying regular series models. The names Team Convoy and Team Matchbox are essentially interchangeable names given to a series of racing sets featuring variations of CY – 10 Race Car Transporter. Sets are valued around $6.00 each if in mint condition with original container (MOC).

"DAYS OF THUNDER"

The movie "Days of Thunder," starring Tom Cruise, stimulated many promotional items, including this series from Matchbox. Items include Chevrolet Luminas with marking similar to those in the motion picture. Sets include variations of CY – 19 Peterbilt Box Car and matching Lumina, or CY – 10 Race Car Transporter with matching car. Note that individual Luminas, while packaged as Matchbox models, are actually manufactured by Racing Champions, an independent company that specializes in racing toys and models. Individual race cars are valued around $3.00 each. Transport sets are valued around $7.00 each.

"INDY 500" SETS

Another racing promotional for 1991, these models and sets include 16 – H or 65 – G racers in different colors and marking variations, as well as accompanying CY – 10 transporters in sets. New variations in model combinations, colors and markings expand on the series in 1992. Individual race cars are valued around $3.00 each. Transport sets are valued around $7.00 each.

Many other promotional sets have been produced from time to time, and a special section at the end of this book deals briefly with the latest items as indicated in the 1992 Dealer Catalog.

SKY BUSTERS

These small scale aircraft, typically about 3½ inches long, were introduced in 1973. Current models are available for around $4.00 each and are divided into two groups for marketing purposes as either Commercial or Military models. These are typically 3½" long.

MODEL NUMBER	MODEL DESCRIPTION
1973	
SB – 1 – A	Learjet
SB – 2 – A	Corsair A7D
SB – 3 – A	A300B Airbus
SB – 4 – A	Mirage F1
SB – 5 – A	Starfighter
SB – 6 – A	MIG 21
SB – 7 – A	Junkers 87B
SB – 8 – A	Spitfire
SB – 9 – A	Cessna 420
SB – 10 – A	Boeing 747
SB – 11 – A	Alpha Jet
SB – 12 – A	Douglas Skyhawk
SB – 13 – A	DC-10
SB – 14 – A	Cessna 210
1975	
SB – 15 – A	Phantom F4E
SB – 16 – A	Corsair F4U
1976	
SB – 17 – A	Ram Rod
SB – 18 – A	Wild Wind
1977	
SB – 19 – A	Piper Comanche
SB – 20 – A	Helicopter
SB – 21 – A	Lightning
1978	
SB – 22 – A	Tornado
1979	
SB – 23 – A	SST Super Sonic Transport
SB – 24 – A	F-16

MODEL NUMBER	MODEL DESCRIPTION
SB – 25 – A	Rescue Helicopter
1980	
SB – 3 – B	NASA Space Shuttle
SB – 12 – B	Pitts Special Biplane
1981	
SB – 26 – A	Cessna 210 Float Plane
SB – 27 – A	Harrier Jet
SB – 28 – A	A300 Airbus
1989	
SB – 29 – A	Lockheed SR-71 Blackbird
SB – 30 – A	Grumman F-14 Tomcat
1990	
SB – 26 – B	Lockheed F-117A Stealth (also see SB – 36 – A, 1991)
SB – 31 – A	Boeing 747-400
SB – 32 – A	Fairchild A10 Thunderbolt (dubbed "Warthog" in the Persian Gulf War)
SB – 33 – A	Bell Jet Ranger Helicopter
SB – 34 – A	Lockheed A130 Hercules
SB – 35 – A	MIL Mi Hind-D Chopper
1991	
SB – 36 – A	Lockheed F-117A Stealth (also see SB – 26 – B, 1990)
1992	
SB – 12 – C	Mission Chopper (variation of 46 – I and 57 – I)
SB – 37 – A	Hawk
SB – 38 – A	B.AE 146
SB – 39 – A	Boeing Stearman Biplane
SB – 40 – A	Boeing 737-300

MAJOR PACK SERIES

The Major Pack series was started by Lesney Products in 1957 in an attempt to capture a new market by producing larger, more detailed models than the regular 1 – 75 series.

In 1960 Lesney introduced a similar series called King Size that ultimately replaced the Major Pack models. A few Major Pack models, however, survived the demise of the series in 1967 by being converted to King Size models. M – 8 – B Guy Warrior car Transporter became K – 8 – B, M – 4 – B GMC Tractor with Hopper Train became K – 4 – B, and M – 6 – B Racing Car Transporter became K – 5 – B.

MODEL NUMBER	YEAR INTRODUCED	DESCRIPTION	LENGTH	CURRENT VALUE
M – 1 – A	1957	Caterpillar Earth Scraper	4½"	$25.00
M – 1 – B	1961	BP Auto Tanker	4"	$35.00
M – 2 – A	1957	Bedford "WALL'S ICE CREAM" Truck	4⁵⁄₁₆"	$30.00
M – 2 – B	1961	Bedford Tractor and York Trailer	4⅝"	$45.00
M – 3 – A	1959	Thornycroft Antar Tractor with Sanky 50-Ton Tank Transporter and Centurion Mk III Tank	4½"	$40.00
M – 4 – A	1959	Ruston Bucyrus Power Shovel	3⅞"	$30.00
M – 4 – B	1964	GMC Tractor and Fruehauf Hopper Train (later K – 4 – B)	11¼"	$30.00
M – 5 – A	1960	Massey Ferguson Combine Harvester	4⅝"	$45.00
M – 6 – A	1960	Pickford 200-Ton Transporter	11"	$30.00
M – 6 – B	1965	Racing Car Transporter (later K – 5 – B)	5⅛"	$95.00
M – 7 – A	1960	Jennings Cattle Truck	4¾"	$25.00
M – 8 – A	1960	Mobilgas Petrol Tanker	3⅞"	$25.00
M – 8 – B	1964	Guy Warrior Car Transporter (later K – 8 – B)	8¼"	$25.00
M – 9 – A	1962	Cooper-Jarrett Interstate Double Freighter with Henderson Relay Tractor	11⅛"	$40.00
M – 10 – A	1962	Dinkum Dumper	4¼"	$35.00

KING SIZE, SUPER KINGS, & SPEED KINGS

Lesney introduced the King Size series in 1960. When the regular series was converted to SuperFast, King Size became the Speed Kings series; later this series was reintroduced as Super Kings.

The Super Kings series was followed by Battle Kings, Sea Kings, and the futuristic Super Kings Adventure 2000 which was introduced in 1977. In 1991 King Size series was renamed Action Series and divided into Construction, Emergency, and Super Kings.

MODEL NUMBER	YEAR INTRODUCED	DESCRIPTION	LENGTH	CURRENT VALUE
K – 1 – A	1960	Weatherhill Hydraulic Shovel	3¹¹⁄₁₆"	$40.00
K – 1 – B	1964	8-Wheel Tipper Truck	4¼"	$35.00
K – 1 – C	1970	O & K Excavator	4⅞"	$20.00
K – 1 – D	1989	Kremer Porsche CK.5 Racer	4¹⁄₁₆"	$7.00
K – 2 – A	1960	Muir Hill Dumper	3"	$25.00
K – 2 – B	1964	KW Dart Dump Truck	5⅝"	$25.00
K – 2 – C	1969	Scammell Heavy Wreck Truck	4¾"	$45.00
K – 2 – D	1977	Car Recovery Vehicle	4¾"	$15.00
K – 2 – E	1989	Kremer Porsche CK.5 Turbo	4¹⁄₁₆"	$7.00
K – 3 – A	1960	Caterpillar Bulldozer	3⁵⁄₁₆"	$30.00
K – 3 – B	1965	Hatra Tractor Shovel	5⅞"	$25.00
K – 3 – C	1970	Massey Ferguson Tractor and Trailer	8"	$18.00
K – 3 – D	1974	Mod Tractor and Trailer	7¾"	$15.00
K – 3 – E	1980	Grain Transporter	11⅞"	$30.00
K – 3 – F	1989	Ferrari 512 Berlinetta Boxer	4¹¹⁄₁₆"	$7.00
K – 4 – A	1960	International Tractor	2¹³⁄₁₆"	$20.00
K – 4 – B	1967	GMC Tractor and Fruehauf Hopper Train (also see M – 4 – B)	11¼"	$30.00
K – 4 – C	1970	Leyland Tipper	4½"	$30.00
K – 4 – D	1974	Big Tipper	4¹¹⁄₁₆"	$25.00
K – 4 – E	1989	RJ Racing Ferrari 512 BB	4¹¹⁄₁₆"	$7.00
K – 5 – A	1961	Foden Tipper Truck	4¼"	$30.00
K – 5 – B	1967	Racing Car Transporter (previously M – 6 – B)	5"	$35.00
K – 5 – C	1972	Muir Hill Tractor Trailer	9½"	$25.00
K – 5 – D	1989	Lancia Rallye	4⁷⁄₁₆"	$7.00
K – 6 – A	1961	Allis-Chalmers Earth Scraper	5⅞"	$25.00
K – 6 – B	1968	Mercedes Benz-Binz Ambulance	4⅛"	$20.00
K – 6 – C	1971	GMC Cement Mixer	5¾"	$15.00
K – 6 – D	1975	Motorcycle Transporter	4¾"	$12.00
K – 6 – E	1989	ZakSpeed Ford Mustang	5¹⁄₁₆"	$7.00

MODEL NUMBER	YEAR INTRODUCED	DESCRIPTION	LENGTH	CURRENT VALUE
K – 7 – A	1961	Curtiss-Wright Rear Dumper	5¾"	$35.00
K – 7 – B	1967	SD Refuse Truck	4⅝"	$20.00
K – 7 – C	1973	Racing Car Transporter	6⅛"	$15.00
K – 7 – D	1989	ZakSpeed Ford Mustang Turbo	5¹⁄₁₆"	$7.00
K – 8 – A	1962	Prime Mover with Caterpillar Crawler	12½"	$35.00
K – 8 – B	1967	Guy Warrior Car Transporter	8¼"	$25.00
K – 8 – C	1970	Caterpillar Traxcavator	4⅛"	$15.00
K – 8 – D	1980	Animal Transporter	12⁵⁄₁₆"	$20.00
K – 8 – E	1989	Ferrari F40	4⁵⁄₁₆"	$7.00
K – 9 – A	1962	Diesel Road Roller	3¼"	$75.00
K – 9 – B	1967	Matador Combine Harvester	5½"	$20.00
K – 9 – C	1968	Claas Combine Harvester	5½"	$15.00
K – 9 – D	1973	Fire Tender	6⅛"	$10.00
K – 9 – E	1989	Ferrari F40 Racer	4⁵⁄₁₆"	$7.00
K – 10 – A	1963	Aveling-Barford Tractor Shovel	4⅛"	$30.00
K – 10 – B	1967	Pipe Truck	8"	$25.00
K – 10 – C	1976	Car Transporter	10½"	$20.00
K – 10 – D	1981	Bedford Courier Car Transporter	10⁵⁄₁₆"	$15.00
K – 10 – E	1989	Chevrolet Camaro Turbo	4⅝"	$7.00
K – 11 – A	1963	Fordson Tractor and Farm Trailer	6¼"	$30.00
K – 11 – B	1969	DAF Car Transporter	9"	$20.00
K – 11 – C	1976	Tow Truck	5"	$15.00
K – 11 – D	1981	Dodge Delivery Van	5⁵⁄₁₆"	$20.00
K – 11 – E	1989	Porsche 959	4⅜"	$7.00
K – 12 – A	1963	Heavy Breakdown and Wreck Truck	4¾"	$25.00
K – 12 – B	1970	Scammell Crane Truck	6"	$25.00
K – 12 – C	1975	Hercules Mobile Crane	6⅛"	$25.00
K – 12 – E	1989	Porsche 959 Racer	4⅜"	$7.00
K – 13 – A	1963	Foden Ready-Mix Concrete Truck	4½"	$25.00
K – 13 – B	1971	Building Transporter	5¾"	$20.00
K – 13 – C	1976	Aircraft Transporter	8"	$15.00
K – 14 – A	1964	Taylor Jumbo Crane	5"	$25.00
K – 14 – B	1971	Scammell Container Truck	5½"	$20.00
K – 14 – C	1977	Heavy Breakdown Truck	5⅛"	$15.00
K – 15 – A	1964	Merryweather Fire Engine	6"	$30.00
K – 15 – B	1973	The Londoner Bus	4¾"	$20.00

MODEL NUMBER	YEAR INTRODUCED	DESCRIPTION	LENTH	CURRENT VALUE
K – 16 – A	1966	Dodge Tractor with Twin Tippers	11⅞"	$45.00
K – 16 – B	1974	Petrol Tanker	11½"	$25.00
K – 17 – A	1966	Ford Tractor with Dyson Low Loader and Case Tractor	11"	$45.00
K – 17 – B	1974	Scammell Articulated Container Truck	9⅞"	$25.00
K – 18 – A	1966	Dodge Articulated Horse Box	6½"	$35.00
K – 18 – B	1974	Articulated Tipper Truck	8"	$18.00
K – 19 – A	1967	Scammell Tipper Truck	4¾"	$30.00
K – 19 – B	1979	Security Truck	12⅞"	$15.00
K – 20 – A	1968	Tractor Transporter with three tractors	9"	$100.00
K – 20 – B	1973	Cargo Hauler and Pallet Loader	7½"	$20.00
K – 20 – C	1979	Peterbilt Wreck Truck	6⁵⁄₁₆"	$15.00
K – 21 – A	1968	Mercury Cougar	4⅛"	$25.00
K – 21 – B	1971	Mercury Cougar Dragster	4⅛"	$15.00
K – 21 – C	1974	Tractor Transporter	6⅜"	$20.00
K – 21 – D	1979	Ford Transcontinental Double Freighter	11"	$20.00
K – 22 – A	1969	Dodge Charger	4½"	$20.00
K – 22 – B	1971	Dodge Dragster	4½"	$15.00
K – 22 – C	1974	SRN6 Hovercraft	5"	$15.00
K – 23 – A	1969	Mercury Commuter Police Station Wagon	4⅜"	$15.00
K – 23 – B	1974	Scammell Crusader Low Loader with Bulldozer	11"	$35.00
K – 24 – A	1969	Lamborghini Miura	4"	$15.00
K – 24 – B	1977	Scammell Container Truck (see K – 14 – B)	5¼"	$15.00
K – 25 – A	1971	Seaburst Power Boat and Trailer	6"	$25.00
K – 25 – B	1977	Digger and Plough	5⅛"	$15.00
K – 26 – A	1971	Mercedes Benz Ambulance (see K – 6 – B)	4⅛"	$15.00
K – 26 – B	1980	Cement Truck	4"	$15.00
K – 27 – A	1971	Camping Cruiser	4⅜"	$15.00
K – 27 – B	1978	Power Boat and Transporter	10⅛"	$25.00
K – 28 – A	1971	Drag Pack Mercury Commuter and Dodge Dragster	11"	$30.00
K – 28 – B	1978	Skip Truck	4⁵⁄₁₆"	$15.00
K – 29 – A	1971	Miura Seaburst Set	10"	$30.00
K – 29 – B	1978	Ford Delivery Van	4⁵⁄₁₆"	$20.00
K – 30 – A	1977	Mercedes C1.11	4"	$15.00
K – 30 – B	1978	Unimog and Compressor	7¼"	$15.00
K – 31 – A	1972	Bertone Runabout	4"	$15.00
K – 31 – B	1978	Peterbilt Refrigerator Truck	11⅞"	$20.00

MODEL NUMBER	YEAR INTRODUCED	DESCRIPTION	LENGTH	CURRENT VALUE
K – 32 – A	1972	Shovel Nose Custom Car	4"	$12.00
K – 32 – B	1978	Farm Unimog and Livestock Trailer	8⅞"	$15.00
K – 33 – A	1972	Citroen SM	4½"	$15.00
K – 33 – B	1978	Cargo Hauler	8¾"	$15.00
K – 34 – A	1972	Thunderclap Racer	4"	$12.00
K – 34 – B	1979	Pallet Truck and Forklift	5⅝"	$15.00
K – 35 – A	1972	Lightning Custom Car	4¼"	$12.00
K – 35 – B	1979	Massey Ferguson and Hay Trailer	8⅞"	$15.00
K – 36 – A	1972	Bandalero Custom Car	4½"	$13.00
K – 36 – B	1978	Construction Transporter	6⅜"	$20.00
K – 37 – A	1973	Sandcat	3⅜"	$13.00
K – 37 – B	1979	Leyland Tipper	4⁵⁄₁₆"	$15.00
K – 38 – A	1973	Gus' Gulper	4¼"	$13.00
K – 38 – B	1980	Dodge Ambulance	5⁵⁄₁₆"	$20.00
K – 39 – A	1973	Milligan's Mill	4½"	$12.00
K – 39 – B	1980	ERF Simon Snorkel Fire Engine	8¼"	$20.00
K – 40 – A	1973	Blaze Trailer Fire Chief's Car	4"	$13.00
K – 40 – B	1980	Pepsi Delivery Truck	5⁵⁄₁₆"	$15.00
K – 41 – A	1973	Fuzz Buggy	4½"	$13.00
K – 41 – B	1977	Brabham BT44B	4¼"	$10.00
K – 41 – C	1981	JCB Excavator	9⅞"	$18.00
K – 42 – A	1973	Nissan 270ZX	4"	$12.00
K – 42 – B	1979	Caterpillar Traxcavator Road Ripper	5½"	$15.00
K – 43 – A	1973	Cambuster Custom Street Rod	4⅜"	$12.00
K – 43 – B	1981	Log Transporter	12⅝"	$20.00
K – 44 – A	1973	Bazooka Custom Street Rod	4⅜"	$12.00
K – 44 – B	1977	Surtees F1 Racer	4¼"	$10.00
K – 44 – C	1981	Bridge Transporter	13⅛"	$55.00
K – 45 – A	1973	Marauder Racer	4⅛"	$12.00
K – 46 – A	1973	Race Pack Mercury Commuter and Thunderclap Racer	11"	$25.00
K – 47 – A	1973	Easy Rider Motorcycle	4¾"	$12.00
K – 48 – A	1973	Mercedes 350SLC	4⅛"	$15.00
K – 49 – A	1973	Ambulance	4⅜"	$15.00
K – 50 – A	1973	Street Rod	4"	$55.00
K – 51 – A	1973	Barracuda Custom Racer	4¼"	$12.00
K – 52 – A	1974	Datsun Rally Car	4⅛"	$15.00

MODEL NUMBER	YEAR INTRODUCED	DESCRIPTION	LENGTH	CURRENT VALUE
K – 53 – A	1975	Hot Fire Engine	3⅞"	$13.00
K – 54 – A	1975	Javelin AMX	4¼"	$12.00
K – 55 – A	1975	Corvette Caper Cart	4¼"	$10.00
K – 56 – A	1975	Maserati Bora	4"	$15.00
K – 57 – A	1975	Javelin Drag Racing Set	9¾"	$25.00
K – 58 – A	1975	Corvette Power Boat Set	10⅛"	$25.00
K – 59 – A	1976	Ford Capri Mk 2	4⅛"	$10.00
K – 60 – A	1976	Ford Mustang II	4¼"	$15.00
K – 60 – B	1978	Ford Mustang Cobra	4¼"	$12.00
K – 61 – A	1976	Mercedes Police Car	4¼"	$15.00
K – 62 – A	1977	Citroen SM Doctor's Car	4½"	$10.00
K – 63 – A	1977	Mercedes Benz Ambulance (see K – 26 – A)	4⅛"	$12.00
K – 64 – A	1978	Fire Control Range Rover	4⅛"	$12.00
K – 65 – A	1978	Plymouth Trail Duster Rescue Vehicle	4½"	$15.00
K – 66 – A	1978	Jaguar XJ12 Police Set	4¾"	$15.00
K – 67 – A	1978	Dodge Monaco Fire Chief	4½"	$10.00
K – 68 – A	1979	Dodge Monaco and Travel Trailer	8¼"	$30.00
K – 69 – A	1980	Jaguar and Europa Caravan	10⅝"	$30.00
K – 70 – A	1979	Porsche Turbo	4⅝"	$12.00
K – 71 – A	1979	Porsche Polizei	4⅞"	$12.00
K – 72 – A	1980	Brabham BT44B (see K – 41 – B)	4¼"	$10.00
K – 73 – A	1980	Surtees F1 (see K – 44 – B)	4¼"	$10.00
K – 74 – A	1980	Volvo Estate Car	5⅜"	$15.00
K – 75 – A	1980	Airport Rescue Fire Tender	5⁵⁄₁₆"	$15.00
K – 76 – A	1981	Volvo Rally Set	10⅝"	$25.00
K – 77 – A	1980	Highway Rescue Vehicle	5⁵⁄₁₆"	$12.00
K – 78 – A	1979	Gran Fury Police Car	5⅜"	$8.00
K – 78 – B	1990	Gran Fury Fire Chief Car	5⅜"	$6.00
K – 79 – A	1979	Gran Fury Taxi	4⅜"	$8.00
K – 80 – A	1980	Dodge Custom Van	5⁵⁄₁₆"	$10.00
K – 81 – A	1981	Suzuki Motorcycle and Rider	4⁵⁄₁₆"	$8.00
K – 82 – A	1981	BMW Motorcycle and Rider	4⁵⁄₁₆"	$8.00
K – 83 – A	1981	Harley Davidson Motorcycle and Rider	4⁵⁄₁₆"	$12.00
K – 84 – A	1981	Peugeot 305	4½"	$15.00
K – 85 – A		NOT ISSUED		NOT ISSUED
K – 86 – A	1981	Volkswagen Golf		$12.00

MODEL NUMBER	YEAR INTRODUCED	DESCRIPTION	CURRENT VALUE
K – 87 – A	1981	Massey Ferguson Tractor and Rotary Rake	$15.00
K – 88 – A	1981	Money Box	$20.00
K – 89 – A	1982	Forestry Range Rover and Trailer	$25.00
K – 90 – A	1982	Matra Rancho	$22.00
K – 91 – A	1982	Motorcycle Racing Set	$20.00
K – 92 – A	1982	Helicopter Transporter	$15.00
K – 93 – A	1982	Lamp Maintenance Set	$60.00
K – 94 – A		NOT ISSUED	NOT ISSUED
K – 95 – A	1982	Audi Quattro	$6.00
K – 96 – A	1984	Volvo Ambulance	$8.00
K – 97 – A	1983	Range Rover Police Set	$12.00
K – 98 – A	1979	Forestry Unimog	$8.00
K – 98 – B	1983	Porsche 944	$6.00
K – 99 – A	1979	Range Rover Polizei Set	$12.00
K – 100 – A	1983	Ford Sierra XR4	$8.00
K – 101 – A	1983	Racing Porsche	$8.00
K – 102 – A	1983	Race Rally Support Set	$15.00
K – 103 – A	1983	Peterbilt Tanker	$8.00
K – 104 – A	1983	Matra Rancho Rescue Set	$20.00
K – 105 – A	1985	Peterbilt Tipper	$12.00
K – 106 – A	1984	Aircraft Transporter	$15.00
K – 107 – A	1984	Power Launch Transporter	$16.00
K – 108 – A	1984	Digger and Plough Transporter	$16.00
K – 109 – A	1984	Matra Rancho Rescue Set	$20.00
K – 110 – A	1985	Magirus Deutz Fire Engine	$10.00
K – 111 – A	1985	Peterbilt Refuse Truck	$10.00
K – 112 – A	1985	Fire Spotter Airplane Transporter	$20.00
K – 113 – A	1985	Garage Transporter	$50.00
K – 114 – A	1985	Mobile Crane	$25.00
K – 115 – A	1985	Mercedes Benz 190E 2.3 16V	$8.00
K – 116 – A	1985	Road Construction Set	$25.00
K – 117 – A	1985	Scania Transporter with Traxcavator Bulldozer	$25.00
K – 118 – A	1985	Road Construction Set	$25.00
K – 119 – A	1985	Fire Rescue Set	$25.00
K – 120 – A	1986	Leyland Car Transporter	$20.00
K – 121 – A	1986	Peterbilt Wrecker	$8.00

MODEL NUMBER	YEAR INTRODUCED	DESCRIPTION	CURRENT VALUE
K – 122 – A	1986	DAF Road Train	$20.00
K – 123 – A	1986	Leyland Cement Truck	$8.00
K – 124 – A	1986	Mercedes Container Truck	$10.00
K – 125 – A		NOT ISSUED	NOT ISSUED
K – 126 – A	1986	DAF Helicopter Transporter	$15.00
K – 127 – A	1986	Peterbilt Tanker	$10.00
K – 128 – A	1986	DAF Aircraft Transporter	$16.00
K – 129 – A	1986	Mercedes Power Launch Transporter	$16.00
K – 130 – A	1986	Peterbilt Digger Transporter	$16.00
K – 131 – A	1986	Iveco Petrol Tanker	$12.00
K – 132 – A	1986	Magirus Deutz Fire Engine	$10.00
K – 133 – A	1986	Iveco Refuse Truck	$10.00
K – 134 – A	1986	Fire Spotter Airplane Transporter	$20.00
K – 135 – A	1986	Mercedes Garage Transporter	$50.00
K – 136 – A	1986	Iveco Racing Car Transporter FERRARI	$20.00
K – 137 – A	1986	Road Construction Set	$25.00
K – 138 – A	1986	Fire Rescue Set	$25.00
K – 139 – A	1987	Iveco Tipper Truck	$10.00
K – 140 – A	1987	Leyland Car Recovery Vehicle	$12.00
K – 141 – A	1987	Leyland Skip Truck	$8.00
K – 142 – A	1987	BMW Police Car	$8.00
K – 143 – A	1987	Emergency Van	$10.00
K – 144 – A	1987	Land Rover Pilot Car	$10.00
K – 145 – A	1988	Iveco Double Tipper	$16.00
K – 146 – A	1988	Jaguar XJ6	$6.00
K – 147 – A	1988	BMW 7-Series 720il	$6.00
K – 148 – A	1988	Mercedes Crane Truck	$20.00
K – 149 – A	1988	Ferrari Testarossa	$6.00
K – 150 – A	1988	Leyland Truck with three interchangeable backs	$12.00
K – 151 – A	1988	Leyland Skip Truck	$8.00
K – 152 – A		NOT ISSUED	NOT ISSUED
K – 153 – A	1988	Jaguar XJ6 Police Car	$6.00
K – 154 – A	1988	BMW 7-Series 720il Police Car	$6.00
K – 155 – A	1988	Ferrari Testarossa	$6.00
K – 156 – A	1988	Porsche Turbo 944	$6.00
K – 157 – A	1988	Porsche Turbo 944 Racer	$6.00

MODEL NUMBER	YEAR INTRODUCED	DESCRIPTION	CURRENT VALUE
K – 158 – A	1988	Ford Sierra XR4i	$6.00
K – 159 – A	1988	Porsche Racing Car Transporter	$15.00
K – 160 – A	1989	Matchbox Racing Car Transporter	$15.00
K – 161 – A	1989	Rolls Royce Silver Spirit	$6.00
K – 162 – A	1989	Ford Sierra RS500 Cogsworth	$10.00
K – 163 – A	1989	Unimog Snow Plow	$12.00
K – 164 – A	1989	Range Rover	$12.00
K – 165 – A	1989	Range Rover Police	$12.00
K – 166 – A	1989	Mercedes Benz 190E Taxi	$8.00
K – 167 – A	1989	Ford Transit Van	$10.00
K – 168 – A	1989	Porsche 911	$6.00
K – 169 – A	1989	Ford Transit Ambulance	$10.00
K – 170 – A	1989	JCB 808 Excavator	$16.00
K – 171 – A	1989	Toyota 4x4 Hi-Lux	$8.00
K – 172 – A	1991	Mercedes Benz 500 SL	$6.00
K – 173 – A	1992	Lamborghini Diablo	$6.00
K – 174 – A		NOT ISSUED	NOT ISSUED
K – 175 – A		NOT ISSUED	NOT ISSUED
K – 176 – A		NOT ISSUED	NOT ISSUED
K – 177 – A		NOT ISSUED	NOT ISSUED
K – 178 – A		NOT ISSUED	NOT ISSUED
K – 179 – A	1992	Suzuki Santana	$8.00

In 1992 the SuperKings were introduced. This listing only shows two examples, K – 173 – A and K – 179 – A.

ACTION SERIES

In 1992 the King Size series was broken down into four groups and renamed Action series. The groups are Action Farming, Construction, Emergency and SuperKings. SuperKings is a random assortment of previous released models. The only new 1991 model for this group is K – 172 – A Mercedes Benz 500SL. The only new models for 1992 are K – 173 – A Lamborghini Diablo and K – 179 – A Suzuki Santana.

MODEL NUMBER	MODEL DESCRIPTION	CURRENT VALUE
ACTION FARMING		
FM – 1	Range Rover with sheep, shepherd, and dog	$8.00
FM – 2	Muir Tractor and Back Shovel	$8.00
FM – 3	Shovel Tractor with ducks, chicken, and rooster	$8.00
FM – 4	Toyota Hi-Lux with milk cans and cow	$8.00
FM – 5	Muir Tractor and Back Shovel with trailer	$12.00
FM – 6	Massey Ferguson, red with hay trailer	$12.00
FM – 7	Massey Ferguson, green with hay rake	$12.00
FM – 8	Farm Set Massey Ferguson Tractor with accessories	$18.00
CONSTRUCTION (All models in red and yellow)		
CS – 1	Bulldozer	$8.00
CS – 2	Ford Transit	$8.00
CS – 3	Leyland Cement Truck	$8.00
CS – 4	Leyland Skip Truck	$8.00
CS – 5	Unimog Tar Sprayer	$8.00
CS – 6	Iveco Tipper Truck	$8.00
CS – 7	Digger and Plough	$8.00
CS – 8	Mobile Crane	$12.00
CS – 9	JCB 808 Excavator	$8.00

MODEL NUMBER	MODEL DESCRIPTION	CURRENT VALUE
CS – 10	Scania Digger Transporter	$12.00
CS – 11	Mercedes Pipe Transporter	$12.00
EMERGENCY		
EM – 1	Gran Fury U.S. Police Car (yellow)	$6.00
EM – 2	Matra Rancho "FIRE CONTROL UNIT" (red)	$8.00
EM – 3	Jaguar XJ6 Police	$6.00
EM – 4	BMW 730 Polizei/Police	$6.00
EM – 5	Iveco Fire Engine	$8.00
EM – 6	Range Rover Police	$8.00
EM – 7	Ford Transit Ambulance	$8.00
EM– 8	Peterbilt Wreck Truck and Porsche 959	$12.00
EM – 9	DAF Helicopter Transporter "COAST GUARD"	$12.00
EM – 10	Snorkel Fire Engine	$12.00
EM – 11	Fire Spotter Plane Transporter	$12.00
EM – 12	Mercedes Power Launch Transporter	$12.00
EM – 13	Helicopter	$8.00
EM – 14	Suzuki Santana Police	$8.00
EM – 50	Emergency Set Snorkel Fire Engine, Fire Spotter Plane, BMW 730 Police, Helicopter, Ford Transit Ambulance and Accessories	$45.00

MATCHBOX MILITARY & BATTLE KINGS

The Battle Kings series originated in Germany and South Africa as the test market for the series originally called Matchbox Military which was introduced in 1973. The name Battle Kings was originated in 1974.

MODEL NUMBER	YEAR INTRODUCED	DESCRIPTION	LENGTH	CURRENT VALUE
MATCHBOX MILITARY				
MM – 1	1973	Articulated Petrol Tanker (South Africa and Germany only)	8"	$16.00
MM – 2	1973	Armored Car Transporter (South Africa and Germany only)	7½"	$16.00

MODEL NUMBER	YEAR INTRODUCED	DESCRIPTION	LENGTH	CURRENT VALUE
BATTLE KINGS				
BK – 101	1974	Sherman Tank	3⅝"	$12.00
BK – 102	1974	M48A2 Tank	4⅝"	$12.00
BK – 103	1974	Chieftain Tank	4¾"	$12.00
BK – 104	1974	King Tiger Tank	4½"	$12.00
BK – 105	1974	Hover Raider	4⅞"	$20.00
BK – 106	1974	Tank Transporter with M48A2 Tank	10½"	$20.00
BK – 107	1974	155mm S.P. Howitzer	4¼"	$12.00
BK – 108	1974	M3A1 Half Track APC	3⅞"	$12.00
BK – 109	1975	M551 Sheridan Tank	4⅛"	$12.00
BK – 110	1975	Recovery Vehicle	5⅛"	$12.00
BK – 111	1975	Missile Launcher	4⅜"	$15.00
BK – 112	1977	DAF Ambulance	3¾"	$12.00
BK – 113	1977	Military Crane Truck	6⅛"	$15.00
BK – 114	1977	Army Aircraft Transporter	8"	$15.00
BK – 115	1977	Army Petrol Tanker	9"	$12.00
BK – 116	1977	Troop carrier with 226mm Howitzer	8⅞"	$20.00
BK – 117	1977	Self Propelled Rocket Launcher	4⅛"	$15.00

SEA KINGS

In 1976 a line of military ship models was introduced and named Sea Kings. The series, however, was short lived and only produced 10 models.

MODEL NUMBER	YEAR INTRODUCED	DESCRIPTION	LENGTH	CURRENT VALUE
SK – 301	1976	Frigate	8⅝"	$12.00
SK – 302	1976	Corvette	7⅞"	$12.00
SK – 303	1976	Battleship	8½"	$12.00
SK – 304	1976	Aircraft Carrier	8¾"	$12.00
SK – 305	1976	Submarine Chaser	7⅞"	$12.00
SK – 306	1976	Convoy Escort	7⅞"	$12.00
SK – 307	1976	Helicopter Carrier	8¼"	$12.00
SK – 308	1976	Guided Missile Destroyer	8¹⁵⁄₁₆"	$12.00

ADVENTURE 2000

This series consists of futuristic vehicles which were introduced in 1977. The series consists of four vehicles and a set.

MODEL NUMBER	YEAR INTRODUCED	DESCRIPTION	LENGTH	CURRENT VALUE
K – 2001	1977	Raider Commander	6⁵⁄₁₆"	$20.00
K – 2002	1977	Flight Hunter	4¹³⁄₁₆"	$20.00
K – 2003	1977	Crusader Tank	4⅜"	$20.00
K – 2004	1977	Rocket Striker	4⅜"	$20.00
K – 2005	1977	Command Force – Set of four vehicles		$40.00
		Includes: 68 – D Cosmobile	3"	
		59 – F Planet Scout	3"	
		2 – G Hovercraft	3"	
		K – 2004 Rocket Striker	4⅜"	
K – 2006	1982	Shuttle Launcher	4⅜"	$30.00

MODELS OF YESTERYEAR

The success of the original 1 – 75 series of Matchbox models by Lesney prompted the introduction in 1956 of Models of Yesteryear. These are slightly larger scale replicas of antique and vintage vehicles. This series continues to be a favorite with collectors worldwide.

MODEL NUMBER	YEAR INTRODUCED	DESCRIPTION	CURRENT VALUE
Y – 1 – A	1956	1926 Allchin Traction Machine	$65.00
Y – 1 – B	1965	1911 Ford Model T	$30.00
Y – 1 – C	1977	1936 Jaguar SS100	$30.00
Y – 2 – A	1956	1911 B Type London Bus	$90.00
Y – 2 – B	1963	1911 Renault 2-Seater	$25.00
Y – 2 – C	1970	1914 Prince Henry Vauxhall	$20.00
Y – 2 – D	1984	1930 4.5 Litre Supercharged Bentley	$18.00
Y – 3 – A	1956	1907 London E Class Tram Car	$60.00
Y – 3 – B	1966	1910 Benz Limousine	$50.00
Y – 3 – C	1974	1934 Ripley MPH	$25.00
Y – 3 – D	1982	1912 Ford Model T Tanker	$18.00
Y – 4 – A	1956	Sentinel Steam Wagon	$135.00
Y – 4 – B	1960	Shand-Mason Horse Drawn Fire Engine	$125.00
Y – 4 – C	1966	1909 Opel Coupe	$35.00
Y – 4 – D	1976	1930 Deusenberg Model J Town Car	$40.00

MODEL NUMBER	YEAR INTRODUCED	DESCRIPTION	CURRENT VALUE
Y – 5 – A	1958	1929 LeMans Bentley	$40.00
Y – 5 – B	1962	1929 4½ Litre S Bentley	$40.00
Y – 5 – C	1969	1907 Peugeot	$25.00
Y – 5 – D	1978	1927 Talbot Van	$25.00
Y – 5 – E	1989	1929 Leyland Titan TD1 London Bus	$18.00
Y – 6 – A	1958	1916 A.E.C. Y Type Lorry	$80.00
Y – 6 – B	1961	1923 Type 35 Bugatti	$45.00
Y – 6 – C	1967	1913 Cadillac	$50.00
Y – 6 – D	1977	1920 Rolls Royce Fire Engine	$25.00
Y – 6 – E	1988	1913 Mercedes Truck "Stuttgarter"	$18.00
Y – 7 – A	1957	4-Ton Leyland Van	$70.00
Y – 7 – B	1961	1913 Mercer Raceabout	$35.00
Y – 7 – C	1968	1912 Rolls Royce	$30.00
Y – 7 – D	1984	1930 Ford Model A Breakdown Truck	$18.00
Y – 8 – A	1958	1926 Morris Cowley "Bullnose"	$80.00
Y – 8 – B	1962	Sunbeam Motorcycle and Milford Sidecar	$55.00
Y – 8 – C	1969	1914 Stutz	$35.00
Y – 8 – D	1978	1945 MG TC	$25.00
Y – 8 – E	1987	1917 Yorkshire Steam Wagon Type WA	$18.00
Y – 9 – A	1958	1924 Fowler "Big Lion" Showman's Engine	$80.00
Y – 9 – Ba	1968	1912 Simplex	$30.00
Y – 9 – Bb	1986	1912 Simplex with display facade	$80.00
Y – 9 – C	1989	1936 Leyland Cub Hook and Ladder Truck	$35.00
Y – 10 – A	1958	1908 "Grand Prix" Mercedes	$100.00
Y – 10 – B	1963	1928 Mercedes Benz 36/220	$80.00
Y – 10 – C	1969	1906 Rolls Royce Silver Ghost	$35.00
Y – 10 – D	1986	1957 Maserati 250F	$18.00
Y – 11 – A	1958	1920 Aveling & Porter Steam Roller	$65.00
Y – 11 – B	1964	1912 Packard Landaulet	$30.00
Y – 11 – C	1973	1938 Lagonda Drophead Coupe	$25.00
Y – 11 – D	1987	1932 Bugatti Type 35	$18.00
Y – 12 – A	1959	1899 London Horse Drawn Bus	$75.00
Y – 12 – B	1967	1909 Thomas Flyabout	$30.00
Y – 12 – C	1979	1912 Ford Model T Truck	$25.00
Y – 12 – D	1988	1937 GMC Van "GOBLIN VACUUM CLEANERS"	$18.00
Y – 13 – A	1959	1862 American "General" Locomotive	$65.00

MODEL NUMBER	YEAR INTRODUCED	DESCRIPTION	CURRENT VALUE
Y – 13 – B	1966	1911 Daimler	$50.00
Y – 13 – C	1973	1918 Crossley R.A.F. Tender	$30.00
Y – 14 – A	1959	1903 "Duke of Connaught" Locomotive	$150.00
Y – 14 – B	1965	1911 Maxwell Roadster	$40.00
Y – 14 – C	1974	1931 Stutz Bearcat	$20.00
Y – 14 – D	1986	1936 E.R.A. "Remus"	$18.00
Y – 15 – A	1960	1907 Rolls Royce Silver Ghost	$35.00
Y – 15 – B	1969	1930 Packard Victoria	$25.00
Y – 15 – C	1987	1920 London Tram	$18.00
Y – 16 – A	1961	1904 Spyker	$45.00
Y – 16 – B	1972	1928 Mercedes Benz SS Coupe	$40.00
Y – 16 – C	1986	1957 Ferrari Dino 246/V12	$18.00
Y – 16 – D	1989	Scammell 100-Ton Truck with Steam Engine	$50.00
Y – 17 – Aa	1973	1938 Hispano Suiza	$20.00
Y – 17 – Ab	1986	1938 Hispano Suiza with display facade	$80.00
Y – 18 – A	1979	1937 Cord 812	$20.00
Y – 18 – B	1986	1920 Atkinson Steam Wagon	$18.00
Y – 19 – A	1980	1933 Auburn 851 "Boattail" Speedster	$20.00
Y – 19 – B	1987	1929 Morris 10 CWT Van	$18.00
Y – 20 – A	1981	1937 Mercedes Benz 540K	$20.00
Y – 21 – A	1981	1929 Ford Model A "Woody" Wagon	$20.00
Y – 21 – B	1989	Ford TT Van "O FOR AN OSRAM"	$18.00
Y – 22 – A	1982	1930 Model A Ford Van	$18.00
Y – 23 – A	1982	1922 A.E.C. S Type Omnibus	$24.00
Y – 23 – B	1989	1930 Mack Tracker	$18.00
Y – 24 – A	1983	1927 Bugatti T44	$20.00
Y – 25 – A	1983	1910 Renault Type AG	$20.00
Y – 26 – A	1984	1918 Crossley Beer Lorry	$18.00
Y – 27 – A	1985	1922 Foden Steam Lorry	$18.00
Y – 28 – A	1984	1907 Unic Taxi	$18.00
Y – 29 – A	1985	1919 Walker Van	$30.00
Y – 30 – A	1985	1920 Mack Truck	$18.00
Y – 31 – A	1990	1933 Morris Pantechicon Van	$20.00
Y – 32 – A	1990	1917 Yorkshire Steam Lorry	$18.00
Y – 33 – A	1990	1920 Mack Truck	$18.00
Y – 34 – A	1990	1933 Cadillac 452 V-16	$18.00

MODEL NUMBER	YEAR INTRODUCED	DESCRIPTION	CURRENT VALUE
Y – 35 – A	1990	1930 Ford Pickup Truck	$18.00
Y – 36 – A	1990	1926 Rolls Royce Phantom I	$18.00
Y – 37 – A	1990	1931 Garret Steam Truck	$18.00
Y – 38 – A	1990	1920 Rolls Royce Armored Car	$35.00
Y – 39 – A	1990	1820 Royal Mail Horse Drawn Coach	$45.00
Y – 40 – A	1991	1931 Mercedes Benz Type 770	$18.00
Y – 41 – A	1991	1932 Mercedes Truck	$18.00
Y – 42 – A	1991	1938 Albion 6-Wheeler	$30.00
Y – 43 – A	1991	1905 Busch Steam Fire Engine	$40.00
Y – 44 – A	1991	1910 Renault Bus	$20.00
Y – 45 – A	1991	1930 Bugatti Royale	$18.00
Y – 46 – A	1991	1868 Merryweather Fire Engine	$50.00
Y – 47 – A	1991	1929 Morris Van	$18.00
Y – 61 – A	1992	1933 Cadillac Fire Engine	$18.00
Y – 62 – A	1992	1932 Ford Model AA 1½ -Ton Truck	$18.00
Y – 63 – A	1992	1939 Bedford KD Truck	$18.00
Y – 64 – A	1992	1938 Lincoln Zephyr	$18.00
Y – 65 – A	1992	Special Limited Edition Set: 1928 Austin 1928 BMW Dixi 1928 Rosengart	$60.00
Y – 66 – A	1992	Special Limited Edition Her Majesty Queen Elizabeth II's Gold State Coach	$60.00

THE DINKY COLLECTION FROM MATCHBOX

"Dinky" toys have been around since before Lesney and Matchbox. But in 1987 the name and the rights to manufacture Dinky toys was purchased by Matchbox Toys International. The first Dinky toys from Matchbox were nothing more than a number of regular series models with the Dinky name attached, per contractual agreement that Matchbox produce models bearing the name by 1988. But in 1989 the Matchbox Dinky Collection was officially born, featuring detailing, quality, and styling synonymous with the reputation established by Dinky nearly 50 years earlier. These models average 4½ – 5" long.

MODEL NUMBER	MODEL DESCRIPTION	CURRENT VALUE	MODEL NUMBER	MODEL DESCRIPTION	CURRENT VALUE
1989			**1991**		
DY – 1	1967 E-Type Jaguar	$18.00	DY – 20	1965 Triumph TR4A-IRS	$18.00
DY – 2	1957 Chevrolet BelAir	$24.00	DY – 21	1964 Mini Cooper "S"	$18.00
DY – 3	1965 MGB-GT	$18.00	DY – 22	1952 Citroen 15CV	$18.00
DY – 4	1950 Ford E83W10-CWT Van	$18.00	DY – 23	1956 Chevrolet Corvette	$18.00
DY – 5	1957 Ford V-8 Pilot	$18.00	DY – 24	1973 Ferrari Dino 246 GTS	$18.00
DY – 6	1951 Volkswagen Deluxe Sedan	$18.00	DY – 25	1958 Porsche 356A Coupe	$18.00
DY – 7	1959 Cadillac Coupe DeVille	$18.00	DY – 26	1957 Studebaker Golden Hawk	$20.00
DY – 8	1948 Commer 8-CWT Van	$18.00	DY – 27	1957 Chevrolet BelAir Convertible	$24.00
DY – 9	1949 Land Rover Series 1	$18.00	**1992**		
DY – 10	1950 Mercedes Benz Bus	$24.00	DY – 28	1969 Triumph Stag	$18.00
1990			DY – 29	1953 Buick Skylark	$18.00
DY – 11	1948 Tucker Torpedo	$18.00	DY – 30	1956 Austin Healy 100	$18.00
DY – 12	1955 Mercedes Benz 300SL Gullwing	$18.00	DY – 31	1955 Ford Thunderbird	$18.00
DY – 13	1955 Bentley R-Type Continental	$18.00	DY – 32	1957 Citroen 2CV	$18.00
DY – 14	1946 Delahaye 145	$18.00	DY – 903	Special Limited Edition Set with display platform, with Triumph T4A, and Austin Healy	$65.00
DY – 15	1953 Austin A40	$18.00			
DY – 16	1967 Ford Mustang GT 2+2 Fastback Coupe	$20.00	DY – 921	Jaguar E-Type	$45.00
DY – 17	1937 Triumph Dolomite	$18.00	DY – 922	Ferrari 246	$45.00
DY – 18	1967 Jaguar E-Type	$18.00	DY – 923	Chevrolet Corvette	$45.00
DY – 19	1973 MGB-GT V-8	$18.00	DY – 924	Mercedes Benz 300SL Gullwing	$45.00

CATALOGS

The first Matchbox collector catalog, produced in 1958, was no more than a foldout sheet. For later catalogs the form of a pocket-sized booklet became the standard. The standard size, whether horizontally or vertically formatted, was established at roughly 4" x 6". Variations of this size came in the form of specialty catalogs such as the 1990 German Yesteryear/Dinky catalog. This catalog was measured as 8¼" x 5¾". All catalogs are printed in full color.

Values listed below are based on Lt. Col. James W. Smith's September 1992 price list of Matchbox collector catalogs. An avid collector, Smith provides what the author believes to be the best representation of current values available for these catalogs; Smith himself admits that at best his prices are "a matter of guesswork." In his words most sellers "want too much for what they have," and "they don't seem to understand the 'supply and demand' factor."

As with all prices in this book, the values listed below may vary from region to region, or even from collector to collector. Please use this list only as a guide.

For a copy of Smith's most current price list, send LSASE to:

Lt. Col. James W. Smith
431 George Cross Drive
Norman, OK 73069

CATALOG YEAR	COUNTRY OF ORIGIN	CURRENT VALUE	CATALOG YEAR	COUNTRY OF ORIGIN	CURRENT VALUE
1958	United Kingdom	$100.00	1962	USA	$75.00
			1962	Canada	$100.00
1959 – 1	United Kingdom	$100.00	1962	Germany Type A	$100.00
1959 – 2	United Kingdom	$80.00	1962	Germany Type B	$100.00
			1962	France	$100.00
1960 – 1	United Kingdom	$80.00	1962	International	$90.00
1960 – 1	USA	$90.00	1962	Italy	$100.00
1960 – 2	United Kingdom	$80.00			
1960 – 2	USA	$80.00	1963	United Kingdom	$40.00
			1963	USA	$40.00
1961	United Kingdom	$45.00	1963	France	$80.00
1961	USA	$50.00			
1961	Canada	$80.00	1964	United Kingdom	$50.00
1962	United Kingdom	$75.00	1964	USA	$40.00

CATALOG YEAR	COUNTRY OF ORIGIN	CURRENT VALUE	CATALOG YEAR	COUNTRY OF ORIGIN	CURRENT VALUE
1964	Germany	$75.00	1969 – 1	Italy	$3.00
1964	France	$75.00	1969 – 2	United Kingdom	$5.00
1964	International	$60.00	1969 – 2	USA	$2.50
			1969 – 2	Germany	$8.00
1965	United Kingdom	$45.00	1969 – 2	France	$10.00
1965	USA	$20.00	1969 – 2	International	$2.50
1965	Germany	$45.00	1969 – 2	Italy	$3.00
1965	France	$45.00			
1965	International	$45.00	1970	United Kingdom	$12.50
			1970	USA	$1.50
1966	United Kingdom	$30.00	1970	Germany	$15.00
1966	USA	$15.00	1970	France	$15.00
1966	Germany	$30.00	1970	International	$6.00
1966	France	$30.00	1970	Japan	$18.00
1966	Canada	$30.00	1970	Italy	$2.50
1966	International	$20.00	1970	Spain	$18.00
1966	Japan	$30.00			
			1971	United Kingdom	$4.50
1967	United Kingdom	$20.00	1971	USA	$1.25
1967	USA	$4.00	1971	Germany	$7.00
1967	Germany	$25.00	1971	France	$15.00
1967	International	$10.00	1971	International	$8.00
1967	Japan	$25.00	1971	Japan	$12.00
			1971	Italy	$10.00
1968	United Kingdom	$17.50	1971	Spain	$25.00
1968	USA a. (K – 18 priced @ $2.50)	$2.50	1971	Netherlands	$12.00
1968	USA b. (K – 18 priced @ $3.50)	$1.50			
1968	Germany	$25.00	1972	United Kingdom	$15.00
			1972	USA	$1.25
1969 – 1	United Kingdom (K – 23 sedan)	$25.00	1972	Germany	$20.00
1969 – 1	United Kingdom (K – 23 wagon)	$20.00	1972	France	$18.00
1969 – 1	USA	$1.50	1972	International	$7.50
1969 – 1	Germany	$3.00	1972	Japan	$15.00
1969 – 1	France	$8.00	1972	Italy	$15.00
1969 – 1	International	$5.00	1972	Spain	$15.00
1969 – 1	Japan	$10.00	1972	Netherlands	$15.00

CATALOG YEAR	COUNTRY OF ORIGIN	CURRENT VALUE	CATALOG YEAR	COUNTRY OF ORIGIN	CURRENT VALUE
1972	Norway	$25.00	1976	Germany	$10.00
			1976	France	$12.00
1973	United Kingdom	$6.00	1976	Japan	$12.00
1973	USA	$1.25	1976	Italy	$12.00
1973	Germany	$10.00	1976	Spain	$12.00
1973	France	$8.00	1976	Netherlands	$12.00
1973	International	$15.00	1976	Sweden	$12.00
1973	Japan	$30.00	1976	East Germany	$25.00
1973	Italy	$5.00			
1973	Spain	$5.00	1977	United Kingdom	$7.50
1973	Netherlands	$5.00	1977	USA	$2.00
1973	Norway	$5.00	1977	Germany	$15.00
			1977	France	$10.00
1974	United Kingdom	$5.00	1977	Japan	$10.00
1974	USA	$2.50	1977	Italy	$10.00
1974	Germany	$5.00	1977	Netherlands	$10.00
1974	France	$10.00	1977	Sweden	$25.00
1974	Japan	$20.00	1977	East Germany	$20.00
1974	Italy	$12.00			
1974	Spain	$12.00	1978	United Kingdom	$5.00
1974	Netherlands	$12.00	1978	USA	$1.00
1974	Sweden	$22.50	1978	Germany	$5.00
			1978	France	$7.00
1975	United Kingdom	$10.00	1978	Italy	$7.00
1975	USA	$1.00	1978	Netherlands	$7.00
1975	Germany	$20.00	1978	Sweden	$7.00
1975	France	$12.00	1978	East Germany	$20.00
1975	International	$4.00			
1975	Japan	$12.00	1979 – 80	United Kingdom	$8.00
1975	Italy	$12.00	1979 – 80	USA	$1.00
1975	Netherlands	$12.00	1979 – 80	Germany	$5.00
1975	Sweden	$12.00	1979 – 80	France	$15.00
1975	East Germany	$18.00	1979 – 80	International	$1.50
1976	United Kingdom	$8.00	1979 – 80	Japan	$8.00
1976	USA	$1.50	1979 – 80	Italy	$10.00

CATALOG YEAR	COUNTRY OF ORIGIN	CURRENT VALUE
1979 – 80	Spain	$30.00
1979 – 80	Netherlands	$10.00
1979 – 80	Sweden	$10.00
1979 – 80	East Germany	$20.00
1979 – 80	Denmark	$30.00
1979 – 80	Arabic	$40.00
1980 – 81	United Kingdom	$5.00
1980 – 81	USA	$3.00
1980 – 81	Germany	$5.00
1980 – 81	France	$7.00
1980 – 81	International	$5.00
1980 – 81	Italy	$8.00
1980 – 81	Spain	$8.00
1980 – 81	Netherlands	$8.00
1980 – 81	Sweden	$8.00
1980 – 81	Denmark	$8.00
1981 – 82	United Kingdom	$4.00
1981 – 82	USA	$1.00
1981 – 82	Germany	$4.00
1981 – 82	France	$8.00
1981 – 82	Italy	$8.00
1981 – 82	Netherlands	$10.00
1981 – 82	International	$4.00
1981 – 82	Sweden	$8.00
1981 – 82	Denmark	$8.00
1982 – 83	United Kingdom	$5.00
1982 – 83	USA	$1.00
1982 – 83	Germany	$4.00
1982 – 83	France	$12.50
1982 – 83	Italy	$6.00
1982 – 83	Spain	$5.00
1982 – 83	Netherlands	$5.00
1982 – 83	Sweden	$6.00

CATALOG YEAR	COUNTRY OF ORIGIN	CURRENT VALUE
1982 – 83	Arabic	$17.50
1982 – 83	Finland	$12.00
1983	International	$3.00
1983	Japan	$5.00
1983	Australia	$3.00
1984	International	$4.00
1984	Japan	$5.00
1984	Australia	$3.00
1985	International	$4.00
1985	Germany	$5.00
1985	France	$6.00
1985	Australia	$2.50
1985	Japan (fold-out sheet)	$5.00
1985	Germany Yesteryears	$10.00
1986	International	$2.00
1986	Germany	$5.00
1986	France	$4.00
1986	Netherlands	$4.00
1986	Australia	$3.00
1986	Japan (fold-out sheet)	$4.00
1986	Germany Specialty Catalogs:	
	Yesteryear, Mercedes on cover	$4.00
	Yesteryear, Mercedes on cover (2nd Ed.)	$8.00
	Yesteryear, Red Racer on cover	$4.00
	SuperKing, boy on cover	$5.00
	SuperKing, "1886-1986" on cover	$5.00
	Skybusters	$5.00
1987	International	$3.00
1987	Germany	$5.00
1987	Australia	$4.00
1987	Germany Yesteryear	$4.00

CATALOG YEAR	COUNTRY OF ORIGIN	CURRENT VALUE	CATALOG YEAR	COUNTRY OF ORIGIN	CURRENT VALUE
1987	Japan (fold-out sheet)	$8.50	1989	Italy/Spain Dealer Catalog	$10.00
1988	International	$2.00	1990	International	$2.00
1988	Germany	$4.00	1990	Germany Yesteryear	$3.00
1988	France	NPI			
1988	Germany Yesteryear	$4.00	1991	International	$1.50
1988	Germany Lasers	$2.00	1991	Germany	$3.00
1988	Australia (a height chart)	$5.00	1991	Australia	NPI
1988	Japan (fold-out sheet)	$4.00	1991	Germany Yesteryear/Dinky	$4.00
			1991	Australia Yesteryear/Dinky	$4.00
1989	International	$2.00			
1989	Germany	$3.00	1992	International	NPI
1989	France/Netherlands	$5.00	1992	International Yesteryear	NPI
1989	Spain/Italy	$5.00			
1989	Germany Yesteryear	$3.00			
1989	Italy Yesteryear	NPI			

SECTION THREE: ILLUSTRATED GUIDE

1–75 SERIES MATCHBOX MINIATURES ✠ 900 SERIES, TWO PACKS, TWIN PACKS, TRAILERS

CONVOY SERIES, "DAYS OF THUNDER," & "INDY 500" ✠ KING SIZE SERIES ✠ SEA KINGS

SKY BUSTERS ✠ MODELS OF YESTERYEAR

1 – E Mercedes Benz Lorry and **2 – D** Mercedes
Trailer/1968 $15.00

1 – D Aveling Barford Road Roller/1962
$18.00

1 – G Mod Rod/1971 $10.00

1 – H Dodge Challenger/1976 $4.00

1 – I Revin' Rebel Dodge Challenger/1982
$6.00

1 – J Toyman Dodge Challenger/1983 $4.00

1 – K Jaguar XJ6 Police/1991 $2.00

1 – La Diesel Road Roller
(1988 replica of 1 – A) $10.00

2 – H S-2 Jet/1981 $6.00

Variations of the **2 – I** Pontiac Fiero (bottom) $4.00,
including New Superfast version **SF – 19** (top) $2.00

2 – K Corvette Grand Sport/1988 $2.00

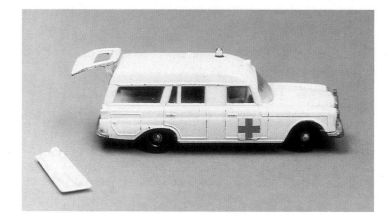

3 – C Mercedes Benz Ambulance/ 1968 $15.00

Five variations of **3 – F** Porsche Turbo 911/1978 $6.00

4 – B Massey Harris Tractor/1957
$60.00

4 – D Dodge Stake Truck/1967 $15.00

Three variations of **4 – H** '57 Chevy $5.00,
including World Class version **WC – 17** (bottom left) $4.00

4 – I Austin London Taxi/1987 $4.00

4 – Ja Massey Harris Tractor/1988 replica
of **4 – A** $10.00

5 – D AEC Routemaster London Bus, "BP
LONGLIFE"/1965 $25.00

5 – G U.S. Mail Jeep/1978 $6.00

Variations of Peterbilt Petrol Tanker: European version **5 – I**
(lower left) $3.00; Two U.S. versions of **56 – G** (top row)
(Note that left one has Peterbilt logo on hood and right one
does not) $4.00; **19 – H** Peterbilt Cement Truck
(bottom right) $5.00

75

Two variations of **6 – F** Mercedes 350SL/1973 $8.00 (right), $2.00 (left)

5 – H Golden Eagle Jeep/1982 $4.00

5 – Ja London Bus/1988 replica of **5 – A** $10.00

6 – C Euclid Quarry Truck/1964 $40.00

7 – B Ford Anglia/1961 $45.00

6 – G IMSA Mazda/1983 $4.00

7 – C Ford Refuse Truck/1966 $20.00

6 – I Ford Supervan II/1985 $3.00

Four variations of the **7 – J** Porsche 959, $2.00, including
M.C. Toys "copycat" version (upper right)

7 – Ka Horse Drawn Milk Cart/1988 replica of
7 – A $10.00

8 – E Ford Mustang Fastback/1966 $16.00

Two variations of the **8 – H** DeTomaso Pantera (bottom) $5.00,
8 – J Greased Lightning DeTomaso Pantera (top) $4.00

8 – I Rover 3500 Police/1982 $8.00

8 – M Mack CH600/1990 $2.00

Two variations of **8 – K** Scania T142/1986 $3.00

9 – E Javelin AMX/1971 $6.00

9 – F Ford Escort RS2000/1978 $6.00

Two variations of **9 – G** Fiat Abarth/1982 $5.00

Two variations of the **9 – I** Toyota MR2 $4.00,
including the New Superfast version **SF – 23**/1987 $2.00

Variations of **58 – F** Faun Dump Truck/1976
(bottom right) $4.00, reissued in 1989 as **9 – K**
Earth Mover (bottom left and top) $2.00

9 – Ja Dennis Fire Escape/1988
replica of **9 – A** $10.00

10 – H Buick LeSabre/1987 $3.00

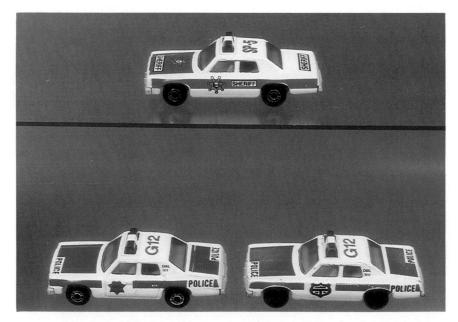

Three variations of **10 – G** Gran Fury Police/1979 $4.00

11 – C Taylor Jumbo Crane/1965 $18.00

11 – G Bedford Car Transporter/1976 $4.00

Two variations of **11 – I** IMSA Mustang/1983 $3.00

12 – G Citroen CX/1979 $6.00

12 – C Safari Land Rover/1965 $45.00

Four variations of **12 – I** Firebird S/E , including New
Superfast version **SF – 2** (upper left and lower right)
$2.00, (upper right and lower left) $5.00

12 – I Firebird S/E New Superfast variation,
SF – 2 – A Halley's Comet
Commemorative Car $5.00

12 – L Mercedes Benz 500SL/1990 $4.00

Five variations of **12 – J** Firebird Racer, $3.00, including New
Superfast variation **SF – 18** (upper left, lower right, and middle)
$2.00

13 – D Dodge BP Wreck Truck/1965 $24.00

13 – G Snorkel Fire Engine/1977 $6.00

14 – L '87 Corvette Convertible/1987 $2.00

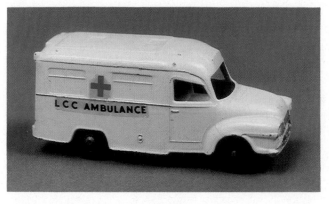

14 – C Bedford Lomas LCC Ambulance/1962
$40.00

14 – D Iso Grifo/1968 $20.00

14 – G Mini HaHa/1975 $6.00

14 – F Rallye Royale/1973 $8.00

86

15 – C Dennis Refuse Truck/1963 $30.00

15 – E Volkswagen 1500 Saloon with Super-fast wheels/1970 $20.00

15 – G Fork Lift Truck/1972 $5.00

15 – J Peugeot 205 Turbo 16/1985 $6.00

15 – K Saab 9000/1988 $4.00

15 – M Alfa Romeo/1991 $2.00

16 – C Scammell Mountaineer Dump
Truck/1964 $75.00

16 – D Case Tractor Bulldozer/1969 $45.00

16 – E Badger Exploration Truck/1974
$12.00

16 – F Pontiac Firebird Trans Am/1979 $4.00

16 – H Formula Racer/1984 $4.00

16 – I Pontiac Trans Am T-Roof/1985 $3.00

16 – J Ford LTD Police/1990 $2.00

17 – D Ergomatic Cab Horse Box/1969 $20.00

Two variations of **17 – F** The Londoner/1972 $15.00 (left),
$8.00 (right)

17 – G The Londoner/1982 (right) $10.00
66 – C Greyhound Bus/1967 (left) $30.00

Four variations of **17 – G** Leyland Titan London Bus/1982
$7.00 each

17 – H AMX Prostocker/1983 $6.00

17 – J Dodge Dakota/1989 $3.00

18 – E Field Car/1969 $25.00,
43 – C Pony Trailer with Superfast wheels/1970 $10.00

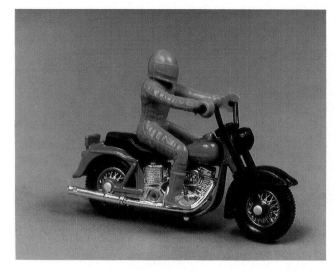

18 – H Extending Ladder Fire Engine/1984
$3.00

18 – G Hondarora Harley Davidson/1975
$8.00

19 – G Badger Cement Truck/1976 $6.00

Two variations of **20 – E** Range Rover Police Patrol/1975
$6.00 each

20 – C Chevrolet Impala Taxi/1965 $32.00

20 – D Lamborghini Marzal/1969 $12.00

20 – H Jeep Laredo/1985 $4.00

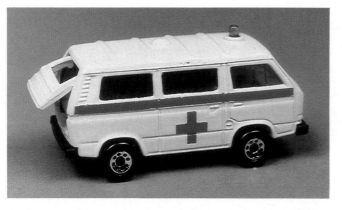

20 – J Volkswagen Vanagon Ambulance/1988
$5.00

21 – C Commer Milk Truck/1961 $35.00

21 – E Foden Concrete Truck with Superfast
wheels/1970 $15.00

21 – G Renault 5TL/1978 $10.00

21 – H Corvette Pace Car/1983 $4.00

21 – I Breakdown Van/1986 $3.00

21 – I Breakdown Van/1986 $3.00

21 – J GMC Wreck Truck/1987 $2.00

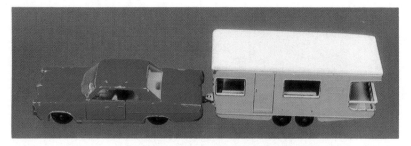

22 – C Pontiac Grand Prix/1964 $18.00
23 – C Trailer Caravan/1965 $20.00

22 – D Pontiac Grand Prix with Superfast wheels/1970
$12.00, **23 – C** Trailer Caravan/1965 $20.00

22 – J Opel Vectra/Chevrolet Cavalier GS/1990
$2.00

22 – Ga Toyota 4x4 Mini Pickup Camper/1982
$4.00

Two variations of **22 – F** Blaze Buster/1975 $6.00 each

23 – G Audi Quattro/1982 $3.00

23 – D Volkswagen Camper with opening roof/1970 $10.00

23 – E Atlas Truck/1975 $4.00

Two variations of **23 – I** Volvo Container Truck/1985 $3.00

24 – C Rolls Royce Silver Shadow/1967 $16.00

24 – D Rolls Royce Silver Shadow with
Superfast wheels/1969 $6.00

24 – H Datsun 280ZX Turbo 2+2, New SuperFast
variation **SF – 9** $2.00

Three versions of the **24 – I** Nissan 300ZX Turbo (bottom) $2.00,
including New Superfast version **SF – 21** (top) $2.00

24 – J Ferrari F40/1989 $2.00

25 – C Bedford BP Petrol Tanker/1964 $30.00

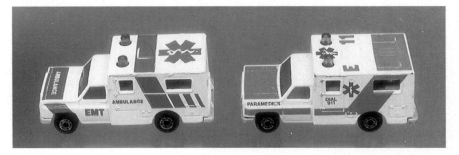

Two variations of **25 – K** Chevrolet Ambulance/1983 $3.00

25 – E Ford Cortina GT in metallic blue with
Superfast wheels/1970 $8.00

25 – D Ford Cortina GT in metallic tan/1968
$20.00

26 – D GMC Tipper Truck with Superfast
wheels/1970 $10.00

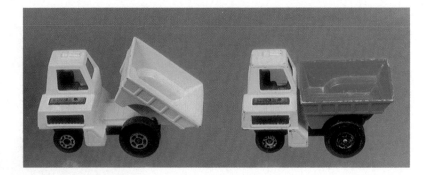

Two variations of **26 – F** Site Dumper/1976 $4.00

26 – G Cosmic Blues/1980 white $4.00, blue $2.00

26 – J BMW 5-Series 535i/1989 $2.00

Two variations of **26 – H** Volvo Tilt Truck/1984 $2.00

27 – D Mercedes 230SL Convertible/1966 $25.00

27 – E Mercedes 230SL Convertible with Superfast
wheels/1970 $15.00

27 – F Lamborghini Countach/1973 $8.00

Three variations of **27 – H** Jeep Cherokee (upper left, lower left, and right)/1987 $2.00; **68 – E** Chevy Vanpire Van (upper right)/1979 $5.00

28 – D Mack Dump Truck/1968 $20.00

28 – C Jaguar Mark 10/1964 $25.00

Five versions of **28 – I** the 1984 Dodge Daytona Turbo Z
$2.00, including New Superfast variation **SF – 4**
(top left and bottom center) $2.00

28 – G Lincoln Continental Mark V/1979 $4.00

28 – M Fork Lift Truck/1991 $2.00

29 – B Austin A55 Cambridge/1961 $36.00,
74 – A Mobile Canteen/1959 $65.00

29 – C Fire Pumper/1966 $20.00

29 – E Racing Mini/1970 $6.00

29 – F Shovel Nose Tractor/1976 $3.00

Two variations of **30 – H** Peterbilt Quarry Truck/1982 $6.00

30 – E Beach Buggy/1971 $12.00

30 – C 8-Wheel Crane Truck/1965 $20.00

30 – I Mercedes Benz 280GE G-Wagon (Commando Strike Team version in rear) 1984 $4.00

31 – C Lincoln Continental in metallic blue/1964
$25.00

Two variations of **31 – H** Mazda RX7/1982 $4.00

31 – J Rover Sterling/1988 $3.00

31 – L Nissan Prairie/1991 $2.00

Two variations of **32 – G** Atlas Excavator/1981 $3.00

32 – E Maserati Bora/1972 $8.00

32 – C Leyland BP Petrol Tanker/1968 $16.00

32 – H Modified Racer/1990 $2.00

32 – H Modified Racer/1990 $2.00

33 – B Ford Zephyr 6 Mk III/1963 $30.00

33 – D Lamborghini Miura with
Superfast wheels/1970 $12.00

33 – E Datsun 126X/1973 $6.00

33 – I Mercury Sable Wagon/1988 $2.00

33 – G Volkswagen Golf GTI/1986 $4.00

34 – A Volkswagen Matchbox
International Express Van/1957 $55.00

33 – J Ford Utility Truck/1989 $2.00

34 – B Volkswagen Camper in light green/1962 $50.00

34 – C Volkswagen Camper with raised roof with windows/1967 $50.00

Three variations of the **34 – I** Chevy Pro Stocker $6.00, including New Superfast versions **SF – 12 – Aa** (lower right) $2.00 and **SF – 12 – Ab** Halley's Comet Commemorative Car (top row) $5.00

Two variations of **34 – J** Ford RS200/1987 $4.00

34 – K Sprint Racer/1990 $2.00

35 – C Merryweather Fire Engine with Superfast
wheels/1969 $15.00

Two variations of **35 – I** Land Rover Ninety/1990 $2.00
each

36 – C Opel Diplomat/1966 $15.00

Four variations of **36 – G** Refuse Truck/1980 $4.00 each

37 – D Dodge Cattle Truck
with two steers/1966 $25.00

37 – I Matra Rancho/1982 $12.00,
57 – IE Eccles Caravan/1970 $3.00

37 – G Atlas Skip Truck/1976 $6.00

37 – J Jeep 4x4/1984 $4.00

38 – A Carrier Refuse Truck in silver/1957
$45.00

37 – J Jeep 4x4/1984 $4.00

Three variations of **38 – H** Ford Model A Van/1982,
top $3.00, bottom $5.00 each

38 – G Camper Pickup/1980 $12.00

Three variations of **39 – E** Rolls Royce Silver Shadow II/ 1979
$8.00 each

39 – F Toyota Celica Supra/1982 $6.00

Two variations of **39 – H** Ford Bronco II 4x4/1990 $2.00 each

Three variations of the **39 – G** BMW 323i
Cabriolet (bottom row) $4.00, including
New Superfast version
SF – 14 (top row) $2.00

40 – B Leyland Royal Tiger Coach/1961
$25.00

40 – D Vauxhall Guildsman/1971 $15.00

40 – F Corvette T-Roof/1982 $8.00

40 – I Road Roller/1991 $2.00

41 – D Ford GT with Superfast wheels/1970 $12.00

41 – E Siva Spider/1972 $8.00

41 – I Jaguar XJ6/1987 $2.00

42 – B Studebaker Lark Wagonaire/1965 $25.00

Three variations of **42 – G** '57 T-Bird/1982 $4.00 each

42 – F Mercedes Container Truck/1977 $6.00

42 – H Faun Mobile Crane/1985 $2.00

43 – F 0-4-0 Steam Locomotive/1978
$10.00, **44 – F** Railway Passenger
Coach/1978 $10.00

43 – J Renault Alliance Turbo II/1987 $2.00

44 – B Rolls Royce Phantom V/1964 $35.00

43 – K Lincoln Town Car/1989 $2.00

Five variations of **43 – I** AMG Mercedes 500SEC $6.00, including
New Superfast version **SF – 5** (top right) $2.00, and World Class
version **WC – 3** (bottom center) $6.00

44 – C GMC Refrigerator Truck/1967 $25.00

Two variations of **44 – G** Chevy 4x4 Van/1982 $4.00 each

44 – I Skoda 130LR Rally/1988 $4.00

44 – H Citroen 15CV/1983 $5.00

44 – J 1921 Ford Model T Van/1990
$2.00

45 – B Ford Corsair/1965
$20.00

45 – D BMW 3.0 CSL/1976 $8.00

45 – C Ford Group 6 with Superfast wheels only/1970
$15.00

123

Four versions of **46 – J** Sauber
Group C Racer $3.00, including
New Superfast version **SF – 16**
(upper right) $2.00

Two variations of **45 – E** Kenworth
Cabover Aerodyne/1982 $3.00 each

PICKFORDS
REMOVERS & STORERS
BRANCHES IN ALL LARGE TOWNS

46 – B Pickfords Removal Van/1960 $60.00

46 – C Mercedes Benz 300SE/1968 $25.00

47 – B Commer Lyons Maid Ice Cream
Truck/1963 $40.00

46 – H Big Blue/1983 $8.00

47 – G Jaguar SS100/1982 $3.00

47 – C DAF Tipper Container Truck/1968 $20.00

48 – G Red Rider/1982 $3.00

47 – H School Bus/1985 $2.00

48 – C Dodge Dump Truck/1966 $20.00

47 – G Jaguar SS100/1982 $3.00

49 – E Crane Truck/1976 $4.00

Two variations of **49 – B** Mercedes Unimog/1967 $20.00 each

48 – I Vauxhall Astra GTE/1987 $6.00

Three variations of the **49 – H** Peugeot Quasar $2.00, including New Superfast version **SF – 25** (lower left) $2.00

50 – E Articulated Truck/1973 $8.00

50 – C Ford Kennel Truck with four dogs/1969 $20.00

51 – C 8-Wheel Tipper Truck, "POINTER" 1969
$15.00

Two variations of **50 – H** Chevy Blazer 4x4 Sheriff/1985
$3.00 each

51 – E Citroen SM/1972 $8.00

Four variations of **51 – J** Camaro IROC Z $2.00, including New Superfast version **SF – 22** (upper right) $2.00

Four variations of **52 – Fa** BMW M1/1982 $4.00 each

Two variations of **53 – Ga** Chevy Flareside Pickup/1982 $4.00 each

52 – C Dodge Charger Mk III with Superfast wheels
only/1970 $12.00

53 – D Ford Zodiac with Superfast wheels/1970 $8.00

53 – F Jeep CJ6/1977 $4.00

54 – G NASA Tracking Vehicle/1982 $4.00

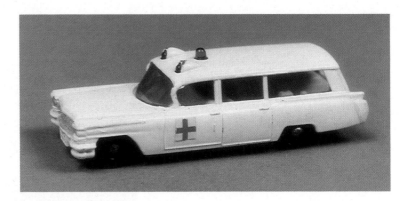

54 – B Cadillac S&S Ambulance/1965 $30.00

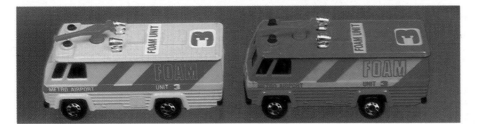

Two variations of **54 – H** Airport Foam Pumper/1985 $2.00

54 – I Chevy Lumina Stock Car/1990 $3.00

55 – H Ford Cortina 1600GL/1979 (left) $4.00,
55 – I Ford Cortina 1600GL/1982 (right) $2.00

55 – C Ford Galaxie Police Car/1966 $30.00

Variations of **55 – K** Ford Sierra XR4 $2.00, including New Superfast
version **SF – 7** (top right) $2.00

More variations of **55 – K** Ford Sierra XR4 (bottom) $2.00,
M.C. Toys "copycat" version (top left) $2.00, **17 – I** Ford Escort XR3
$4.00, New Superfast version **SF – 15** (top right) $2.00

Two variations of **55 – L** Mercury Parklane Police Car including New
SuperFast version **SF – 1** $2.00, and Halley's Comet Commemorative Car $5.00

55 – N Rolls Royce Silver Spirit/1990 $4.00

56 – B Fiat 1500/1965 $25.00

56 – C BMC 1800 Pininfarina with Superfast wheels
only/1970 $10.00

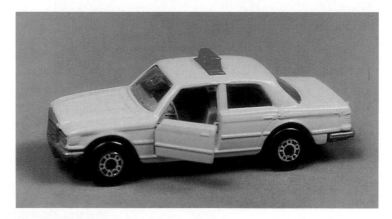

56 – F Mercedes Benz 480 SEL Taxi/1980 $4.00

57 – B Chevrolet Impala/1961 $35.00, **9 – C** Boat and Trailer/1966
$20.00

57 – C Land Rover Fire Truck/1966 $30.00

57 – F Wildlife Truck/1973 $10.00

57 – Hb Mountain Man 4x4 Mini Pickup/1982
$6.00

57 – I Mission Helicopter/1985 $3.00

136

57 – J Ford Transit/1978 $2.00

57 – K Mack Floodlight Heavy Rescue
Auxiliary Power Truck/1991 $2.00

58 – A British European Airways BEA
Coach/1958 $45.00

58 – B Drott Excavator/1963 $30.00

Two variations of **58 – G** Holden Ruff
Trek/1983 $6.00 each

58 – H Mercedes Benz 300E/1987 $2.00

59 – A Ford Thames Singer
Van/1958 $40.00

59 – E Mercury Park Lane Fire Chief with Superfast
wheels/1971 $8.00

Four variations of **59 – G** Porsche 928 $6.00, including New Superfast version **SF – 3** (bottom right) $2.00, M.C. Toys "copy-cat" version (bottom left) $2.00; Note that wheels are identical to Matchbox models.

59 – H T-Bird Turbo Coupe/1988 $2.00

60 – C Leyland Site Office Truck with Superfast wheels/1970 $15.00

60 – Eb Good Vibrations Sunkist Mustang
Piston Popper/1983 $4.00

60 – I NASA Rocket Transporter/1985
$2.00

61 – B Alvis Stalwart BP Exploration Truck/1966
$25.00

Two variations of **61 – E** Peterbilt Wrecker/1982 $4.00 each

61 – G Nissan 300ZX/1990 $2.00

62– C Mercury Cougar/1968 $20.00

62 – E Mercury Cougar Rat Rod/1970 $6.00

62 – F Renault 17TL/1974 $10.00

62 – I Rolls Royce Silver Cloud/1985
$2.00

62 – K Volvo 760/1985 $4.00

63 – C Dodge Crane Truck/1968
$20.00

62 – L Oldsmobile Aerotech/1989 $2.00

63 – E Freeway Gas Tanker/1973 $6.00

Two variations of **63 – H** Snorkel Fire Engine/1982 $3.00 each

63 – I 4x4 Dunes Racer/1987 $2.00

64 – B MG 1100/1966 $20.00

64 – F Caterpillar Bulldozer/1979 $4.00

65 – C Claas Combine Harvester/1967
$15.00

65 – F Tyrone Malone Bandag
Bandit/1982 $2.00

65 – Ea Airport Coach/1977 $10.00

66 – F Ford Transit/1977 $8.00

65 – G Indy Racer/1984 $2.00

67 – B Volkswagen 1600TL/1967 $25.00

66 – G Tyrone Malone Super Boss/1982 $4.00

Four variations of the **67 – E** Datsun 260E 2+2, $8.00 each, including 1991 version with doors that don't open, from the Ten-Value Pack (lower left)

67 – C Volkswagen 1600TL with Superfast wheels/1970 $15.00

Five variations of the **67 – H** Lamborghini Countach LP500S $2.00, including two New SuperFast versions **SF – 17** (top right and bottom center) $2.00

68 – B Mercedes Coach/1965 $30.00 (if base is light
aqua, model is rare: $150.00)

Two variations of **67 – I** Ikarus Coach/1987 $5.00 each

68 – C Porsche 910 with Superfast wheels only/1970 $12.00

Three variations of **68 – F** Dodge Caravan/1985 $2.00 each

69 – A Commer 30 CWT Nestle's Van/1959
$50.00

68 – H Mercedes TV News Truck/1989
$2.00

69 – B Hatra Tractor Shovel/1965
$65.00

69 – C Rolls Royce Silver Shadow Coupe
with Superfast wheels only/1969 $15.00

69 – F 1933 Willys Street Rod/1982
$4.00

69 – E Wells Fargo Armored Truck/1978 $8.00

69 – G 1983 Corvette (right) $2.00, and New Superfast version
SF – 13 1984 Corvette (left) $2.00

69 – H Volvo 480ES/1989 $5.00

69 – I Chevrolet Maintenance Truck/1990 $2.00

70 – A Ford Thames Estate Car/1959 $40.00

70 – B Ford Atkinson Grit Spreader/1966 $30.00

70 – G Ford Skip Truck/1988 $2.00

Four variations of **70 – F** Ferrari 308 GTB $4.00, including New
Superfast version **SF – 11** (bottom left) $2.00

71 – B Jeep Gladiator/1964 $25.00

71 – C Ford Heavy Wrecker "ESSO"/1968 $20.00

Four variations of **71 – G** 1962 Corvette $2.00, including New
Superfast version **SF – 8** (lower left) $2.00

71 – I Porsche 944 Turbo/1988 $2.00

72 – B Standard Jeep/1966 $20.00

72 – H Sand Racer/1984 $2.00

72 – D Hovercraft SRN6/1972 $15.00

72 – I Airplane Trans-
porter/1985 $2.00

Two variations of **72 – L** Cadillac Allante/1988 $2.00

73 – D Mercury Commuter with Superfast wheels/1970
$8.00

73 – G Model A Ford with spare tire cast into fender (top right)
$12.00, **73 – H** Model A Ford with no spare (top left, bottom
left, and right) $6.00

74 – B Daimler Bus "ESSO EXTRA
PETROL"/1966 $30.00

73 – I Mercedes Turbo 1600 Trac-
tor/1990 $2.00

74 – J Williams Honda F1 Grand
Prix Racer/1988 $2.00

74 – E Cougar Villager/1978 $6.00

155

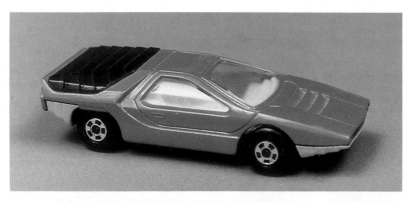

75 – D Alfa Carabo/1971 $10.00

75 – Ba Ferrari Berlinetta with spoked wheels/1965 $40.00

75 – E Seasprite Helicopter/1977 $8.00

75 – F Helicopter/1982 $4.00

Four variations of **75 – G** Ferrari Testarossa $2.00, including New Superfast version **SF – 24** (upper left) $2.00 and M.C. Toys "copy-cat" version (lower right), $1.00

900 SERIES, TWO PACKS, TWIN PACKS, & TRAILERS ━━━

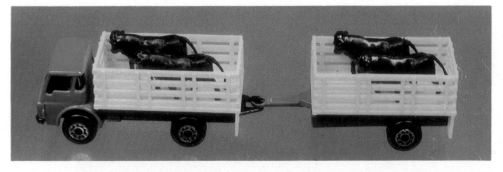

TP – 103 Dodge Cattle Truck and Trailer/1984 $5.00

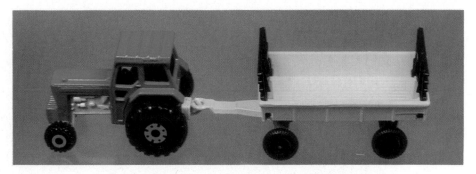

TP – 108 Tractor and Trailer/1984 $5.00

TP – 110 Matra Rancho and Inflatable Raft/1984 $6.00

TP – 112 Unimog and Trailer/1984 $5.00

TP – 115 Ford Escort and Boat/1987 $4.00

TP – 122 Porsche 911 and Glider/1989 $4.00

TP – 123 BMW 323i and Caravan Travel Trailer/1989 $4.00

CONVOY SERIES, "DAYS OF THUNDER" & "INDY 500"

CY – 22 – A DAF Power Boat Transporter (top) $5.00
CY – 13 – A Peterbilt Fire Engine (bottom) $6.00

CY – 15 – B Peterbilt "MBTV News" Remote Truck (top) $5.00
CY – 3 – A Peterbilt Conventional Double Container Truck (bottom)
$12.00

CY – 11 – A Kenworth COE Helicopter Transporter (top) $8.00
CY – 17 – A Scania Petrol Tanker (bottom) $6.00

CY – 1 – A Kenworth COE Car Transporter (top) $12.00
CY – 20 – A Kenworth COE Tipper (bottom) $5.00

Two variations of **CY – 5 – A** Peterbilt Conventional Covered Truck
$12.00

CY – 27 – A DAF Box Car (top) $5.00
"Days of Thunder" Team Transport (bottom) $7.00

KING SIZE SERIES

K – 2 – B KW Dart Dump Truck/1964 $25.00

K – 4 – A McCormick International Tractor/1960 $20.00

K – 4 – B GMC Tractor and Fruehauf Hopper Train/1967 $30.00

K – 9 – D Fire Tender/1973 $10.00

K – 13 – A Foden Ready-Mix Concrete Truck/1963 $25.00

K – 15 – A Merryweather Fire Engine/1964 $30.00

K – 15 – B The Londoner Bus "The Royal Wedding"/1981 $20.00

K – 24 – B Scammell Container Truck/1977 $15.00

K – 33 – A Citroen SM/1972 $15.00

K – 37 – B Leyland Tipper/1979 $15.00

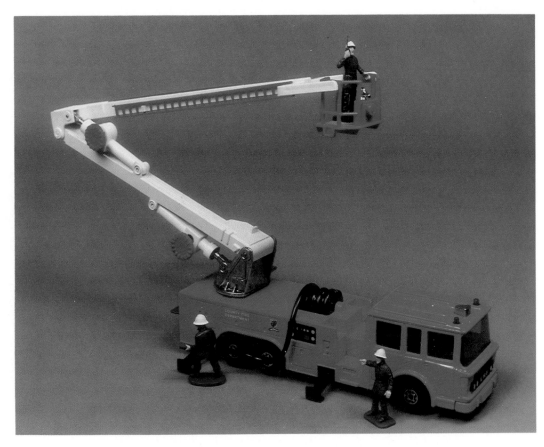

K – 39 – B ERF Simon Snorkel Fire Engine/1980 $20.00

K – 67 – A Dodge Monaco Fire Chief/1978 $10.00

K – 69 – A Europa Caravan (from set with Jaguar XJ12) $30.00

K – 70 – A Porsche Turbo/1979 $12.00

K – 78 – A Gran Fury Police/1979 $8.00

K – 78 – B Gran Fury Fire Chief/1990 $6.00

K – 95 – A Audi Quattro/1982 $6.00

K – 98 – B Porsche 944/1983 $6.00

K – 115 – A Mercedes Benz 190E 2.3 16V/1985 $8.00

K – 121 – A Peterbilt Wrecker/1986 $8.00

K – 123 – A Leyland Cement Truck/1986 $8.00

K – 132 – A Magirus Deutz Fire Engine/1986 $10.00

K – 133 – A Iveco Refuse Truck/1986 $10.00

K – 134 – A Peterbilt Fire Spotter Airplane Transporter/1986 $20.00

K – 139 – A Iveco Tipper Truck/1987 $10.00

K – 141 – A Leyland Auto-Loader Skip Truck/1987 $8.00

K – 146 – A Jaguar XJ6/1988 $6.00

K – 147 – A BMW 70-Series 720il/1988 $6.00

SEA KINGS ━━━━━━━━━━━━━━━━━

SK – 308 Guided Missile Destroyer $12.00

Two variations of **SB – 14** Cessna (top and bottom left) $4.00,
SB – 19 Piper Comanche (top right) $4.00,
SB – 1 Learjet (bottom right) $4.00

SB – 12 Pitts Special (top) $4.00, **SB – 27** Harrier Jet (bottom left)
$4.00, **SB – 24** F16A (bottom right) $4.00

SB – 15 Boeing 747 (top) $4.00,
SB – 20 DC-10 (bottom) $4.00

MODELS OF YESTERYEAR

Y – 1 – B 1911 Ford Model T/1965 $30.00

Y – 1 – B 1911 Ford Model T/1965 $30.00

178

Y – 1 – C 1977 Jaguar SS100/1977 $30.00

Y – 2 – B 1911 Renault 2-Seater/1963 $25.00

Y – 2 – C 1914 Prince Henry Vauxhall/1970 $20.00

Y – 2 – C 1914 Prince Henry Vauxhall/1970 $20.00

179

Y – 3 – A 1907 London E Class Tram Car/1956
$60.00

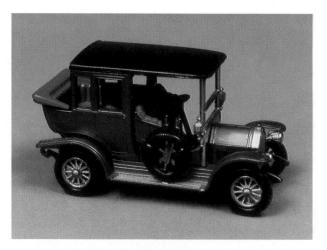

Y – 3 – B 1910 Benz Limousine/1966
$50.00

Y – 3 – C 1934 Riley MPH/1974 $25.00

Y – 3 – D 1912 Model T Tanker/1982 $18.00

Y – 4 – B Shand-Mason Horse Drawn Fire Engine/1960 $125.00 (note: driver missing lowers value to $80.00)

Y – 4 – C 1909 Opel Coupe/1966 $35.00

Y – 4 – D 1930 Deusenberg Model J Town Car/1976 $40.00

Y – 4 – D 1930 Deusenberg Model J Town Car/1976 $20.00

Y – 5 – B 1929 Supercharged 4½ Litre
Bentley/1962 $40.00

Y – 5 – C 1907 Peugeot/1969 $25.00

Y – 5 – C 1907 Peugeot/1969 $25.00

Y – 5 – D 1927 Talbot Van/1978 $25.00

Y – 6 – B 1923 Type 35 Bugatti/1961 $45.00

Y – 5 – D 1927 Talbot Van/1978 $25.00

Y – 6 – D 1920 Rolls Royce Fire
Engine/1977 $25.00

Y – 6 – C 1913 Cadillac/1969 $50.00

Y – 7 – C 1912 Rolls Royce/1968 $30.00

Y – 7 – D 1930 Ford Model A Breakdown
Truck/1984 $18.00

Y – 8 – B 1914 Sunbeam Motorcycle and
Sidecar/1962 $55.00

Y – 8 – C 1914 Stutz/1969 $35.00

Y – 9 – A 1924 Fowler "Big Lion" Show-
man's Engine/1958 $80.00

Y – 9 – Ba 1912 Simplex/1968 $30.00

Y – 8 – D 1945 MG TC/1978 $25.00

Y – 9 – Ba 1912 Simplex/1968 $30.00

185

Y – 10 – B 1928 Mercedes Benz 36/220/1963

Y – 11 – B 1912 Packard
Landaulet/1964 $30.00

Y – 11 – C 1938 Lagonda Drophead
Coupe/1973 $25.00

Y – 12 – A 1899 London Horse Drawn Bus/1959
$75.00

Y – 12 – B 1909 Thomas Flyabout/1967
$30.00

Y – 12 – C 1912 Ford Model T Delivery
Van/1979 $25.00

Y – 12 – C 1912 Ford Model T Delivery
Van/1979 $25.00

Y – 12 – D 1937 GMC Van/1988 $18.00

Y – 13 – B 1911 Daimler/1966 $50.00

Y – 13 – C 1918 Crossley/1973 $30.00

Y – 13 – C 1918 Crossley/1973 $30.00

Y – 14 – B 1911 Maxwell Roadster/1965
$40.00

Y – 14 – C 1931 Stutz Bearcat/1974 $20.00

Y – 15 – A 1907 Rolls Royce Silver
Ghost/1960 $35.00

Y – 15 – B 1930 Packard Victoria/1969 $25.00

Y – 15 – B 1930 Packard Victoria/1969 $25.00

189

Y – 16 – B 1928 Mercedes Benz SS Coupe/1972
$40.00

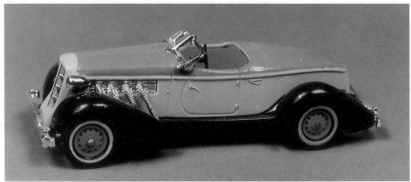

Y – 19 – A 1933 Auburn 851 "Boattail Speedster"/1980
$20.00

Y – 17 – A 1938 Hispano Suiza/1973 $20.00

190

Y – 20 – A 1937 Mercedes Benz 540 K/1981 $20.00

Y – 21 – A 1930 Ford Model A "Woody"
Wagon/1981 $20.00

Y – 22 – A 1930 Ford Model A Van/1982 $18.00

Y – 23 – A 1922 AEC S Type Omnibus/1982 $24.00

Y – 26 – A 1918 Crossley Beer Lorry/1984 $18.00

Y – 30 – A 1920 Mack Model AC/1985 $18.00

Y – 28 – A 1907 Unic Taxi/1984 $18.00

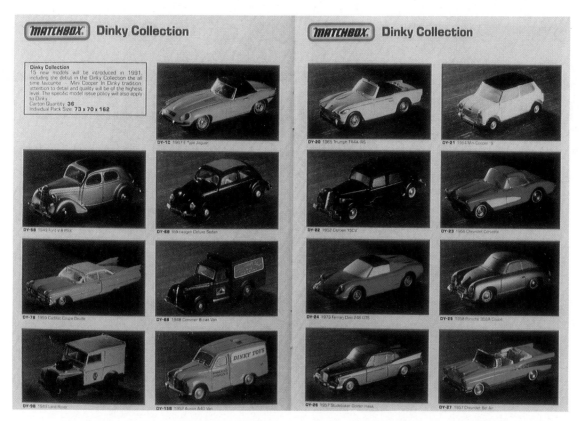

An assortment of **Dinky** models from the 1991 Collectors Catalog.

An assortment of modern packages.

SECTION FOUR:
MATCHBOX MINIATURES 1 – 75 SERIES
INDEX

This index may seem confusing at first compared to the Numerical Price Guide on page 11; however, due to the alphabetical listing of similar model descriptions, we show the year of introduction to lessen the problem. For example; the model 30 – G Articulated Truck is described as a Leyland which was introduced in 1981, while the model 50 – E Articulated Truck was introduced a few years earlier in 1973. Another example is the model 17 – B Austin London Taxi which was introduced in 1960. Then in 1987, the model 4 – I Austin London Taxi was introduced.

MODEL DESCRIPTION	YEAR INTRODUCED	MODEL NUMBER(S)
A		
AEC Ergomatic Cab Dump Truck with regular wheels	1969	51 – C
AEC Ergomatic Cab Dump Truck with SF wheels	1970	51 – D
AEC Ergomatic Cab Horse Box with regular wheels	1969	17 – D
AEC Ergomatic Cab Horse Box with SF wheels	1970	17 – E
AEC Ergomatic 8-Wheel Tipper with regular wheels	1969	51 – C
AEC Ergomatic 8-Wheel Tipper with SF wheels	1970	51 – D
Aerotech, Oldsmobile	1989	62 – L
Alfa Carabo	1971	75 – D
Alfa Romeo	1991	6 – J, 15 – M
Alvis Stalwart "BP EXPLORATION"	1966	61 – B
Airport Coach		
"BRITISH AIRWAYS"	1977	65 – Ea
"AMERICAN AIRWAYS"	1977	65 – Eb
"LUFTHANSA"	1977	65 – Ec
"QUANTAS"	1977	65 – Ed
"SCHULBUS"	1977	65 – Ee
Airport Crash Tender	1964	63 – B
Airport Fire Tender	1992	8 – N
Airport Foam Pumper	1985	54 – H
Albion Chieftain "PORTLAND CEMENT" Truck	1958	51 – A
Ambulance		
Ford Army 3-Ton Service, 4x4	1959	63 – A
Bedford Lomas	1962	14 – C
Cadillac S&S with regular wheels	1965	54 – B
Cadillac S&S with SF wheels	1970	54 – C
Chevrolet Truck, Matchbox INTL	1983	25 – K
Chevrolet Truck, LESNEY	1978	41 – F
Daimler	1956	14 – A
Mercedes Benz with regular wheels	1968	3 – C
Mercedes Benz with SF wheels	1970	3 – D
Volkswagen Vanagon	1988	20 – J
AMG Mercedes Benz 500SEC	1984	43 – I, SF – 5 – A, LW – 5 – A
Amphibian DUKW Army	1959	55 – A
AMX Javelin	1971	9 – E
AMX Pro Stocker	1983	17 – H
Armored Truck, Stoat	1974	28 – F
Armored Truck "WELLS FARGO/DRESDNER"	1978	69 – E
Armoured Car, Saladin	1959	69 – A
Army Halftrack Mk III	1958	49 – A

MODEL DESCRIPTION	YEAR INTRODUCED	MODEL NUMBER(S)
Army Saracen Personnel Carrier	1959	54 – A
Articulated Trailer	1980	50 – F
Articulated Truck	1973	50 – E
Articulated Truck, Leyland	1981	30 – G
Aston Martin DB2 Saloon	1959	53 – A
Aston Martin Racing Car	1961	19 – C
Atkinson Grit Spreader with regular wheels	1966	70 – B
Atkinson Grit Spreader with SF wheels	1970	70 – C
Atlantic Super Truck Tractor	1959	15 – B
Atlantic Trailer	1956	16 – A
Atlantic Trailer	1957	16 – B
Atlas Excavator	1981	32 – G
Atlas Truck	1975	23 – E
Audi Quattro	1982	23 – G
Austin A50	1957	36 – A
Austin A55 Cambridge	1961	29 – B
Austin London Taxi	1960	17 – B
Austin London Taxi	1987	4 – I
Austin Mk 2 Radio Truck	1959	68 – A
Austin 200-Gallon Water Truck	1959	71 – A
Auxiliary Power Truck, Mack Floodlight Heavy Rescue	1991	57 – K
Aveling Barford Road Roller	1962	1 – D
Aveling Barford Tractor Shovel	1962	43 – B

B

Badger Cement Truck	1976	19 – G
Badger Exploration Truck	1974	16 – E
Baja Bouncer Flareside Pickup	1983	53 – Gb
Baja Dune Buggy	1971	13 – F
Bandag Bandit	1982	65 – F
BEA Coach	1959	58 – A
Beach Buggy	1971	30 – E
Beach Hopper	1974	47 – E
Bedford		
Car Transporter	1976	11 – G
Compressor Truck	1956	28 – A
Duplé Long Distance Coach	1956	21 – A
Duplé Long Distance Coach	1958	21 – B
Evening News Van	1957	42 – A
Horse Box	1977	40 – E
Lomas Ambulance	1962	14 – C
Low Loader	1956	27 – A
Low Loader	1959	27 – B
Milk Delivery Van	1956	29 – A
Petrol Tanker	1964	25 – C
Removal Van	1956	17 – A
Tipper Truck	1957	40 – A

MODEL DESCRIPTION	YEAR INTRODUCED	MODEL NUMBER(S)
Ton Tipper	1961	3 – B
12 CWT Dunlop Van	1956	25 – A
Van, Dunlop	1956	25 – A
Van, Evening News	1957	42 – A
Van, Matchbox Removal Service	1956	17 – A
Wreck Truck	1955	13 – A
Wreck Truck	1958	13 – B
Wreck Truck	1993	6 – K
Berkeley Cavalier Travel Trailer	1956	23 – A
Big Banger	1972	26 – E
Big Blue VW	1983	46 – H
Big Bull Bulldozer	1975	12 – F
Bigfoot Toyota Mini Pickup Camper	1983	22 – Gb
Blaze Buster	1975	22 – F
Blazer 4x4 Police	1985	50 – H
Blue Shark	1971	61 – C
Bluebird Dauphine Travel Trailer	1960	23 – B
BMC 1800 Pininfarina	1970	56 – C
BMW		
850i	1993	49 – J
5-Series 535i	1989	26 – J
M1 with opening hood	1981	52 – E
M1 with unopening hood	1982	52 – F
3.0 CSL	1976	45 – D
323i Cabriolet	1985	39 – G, SF – 14 – A, LW – 14 – A
Boss Mustang	1972	44 – B
Boat, Police Launch	1976	52 – D
Boat, Seafire	1975	5 – F
Boat and Trailer		
Meteor Sports Boat, metal boat	1958	48 – A
with regular wheels, plastic boat	1966	9 – C
with SF wheels, plastic boat	1970	9 – D
Bomag Road Roller	1979	72 – F
Breakdown Van	1986	21 – I
Breakdown Truck, Scammell	1959	64 – A
British European Airways Coach	1959	58 – A
BRM Racing Car	1965	52 – B
Brooke Bond Tea Van, Trojan 1 Ton	1958	47 – A
Buick LeSabre	1987	10 – H, SF – 10 – A, LW – 25 – A
Builders Supply Morris J2 Pickup	1959	60 – A
Bulldozer		
Big Bull	1975	12 – F
Case	1969	16 – D
Caterpillar	1955	8 – A
Caterpillar	1959	8 – B
Caterpillar	1961	8 – C
Caterpillar	1964	8 – D

MODEL DESCRIPTION	YEAR INTRODUCED	MODEL NUMBER(S)
Caterpillar	1956	18 – A
Caterpillar	1958	18 – B
Caterpillar	1961	18 – C
Caterpillar	1964	18 – D
Caterpillar	1979	64 – F
Caterpillar Crawler	1964	18 – D
Caterpillar Tractor	1955	8 – A
Caterpillar Tractor	1959	8 – B
Caterpillar Tractor	1961	8 – C
Caterpillar Tractor	1964	8 – D
Bus		
BEA Coach	1959	58 – A
Bedford Duplé Long Distance Coach	1956	21 – A
Bedford Duplé Long Distance Coach	1958	21 – B
British European Airways Coach	1959	58 – A
Daimler with regular wheels	1966	74 – B
Daimler with SF wheels	1970	74 – C
Freeman Inter-City Commuter	1970	22 – E
Greyhound with regular wheels and clear windows	1967	66 – Ca
Greyhound with regular wheels and amber windows	1968	66 – Cb
Greyhound with SF wheels	1970	66 – D
Ikarus	1987	67 – I
Leyland Royal Tiger Coach	1961	40 – B
Leyland Titan London	1972	17 – F
Leyland Titan London	1982	17 – G, 51 – H
London	1954	5 – A
London	1957	5 – B
London	1961	5 – C
London	1965	5 – D
London	1972	17 – F
London	1982	17 – G, 51 – H
London	1959	56 – A
London Trolley	1959	56 – A
The Londoner	1972	17 – F
The Londoner	1982	17 – G, 51 – H
School	1985	47 – H
Setra Coach	1970	12 – E

C

MODEL DESCRIPTION	YEAR INTRODUCED	MODEL NUMBER(S)
Cable Truck, Volvo	1984	26 – I
Cadillac		
Allante	1988	72 – L, SF – 12 – B, LW – 26 – A
S&S Ambulance with regular wheels	1965	54 – B
S&S Ambulance with SF wheels	1970	54 – C
Sixty Special	1960	27 – C
Camaro, IROC Z	1985	51 – I, SF – 22 – A, LW – 21 – A
Camper Pickup Truck	1980	38 – G

MODEL DESCRIPTION	YEAR INTRODUCED	MODEL NUMBER(S)
Camper Pickup Truck, Toyota	1982	22 – G
Car Transporter, Bedford	1976	11 – G
Caravan Travel Trailer	1977	31 – F
Caravan Travel Trailer, Eccles	1970	57 – E
Caravan Dodge	1985	64 – G, 68 – F
Carmichael Commando	1982	57 – G
Case Tractor Bulldozer	1969	16 – D
Caterpillar		
Bulldozer	1956	18 – A
Bulldozer	1958	18 – B
Bulldozer	1961	18 – C
Bulldozer	1964	18 – D
Bulldozer	1979	64 – F
Bulldozer Crawler	1964	18 – D
Bulldozer Tractor	1955	8 – A
Bulldozer Tractor	1959	8 – B
Bulldozer Tractor	1961	8 – C
Bulldozer Tractor	1964	8 – D
Crawler Tractor	1964	18 – D
D8 Bulldozer	1956	18 – A
Tractor	1955	8 – A
Tractor	1959	8 – B
Tractor	1961	8 – C
Tractor	1964	8 – D
Tractor	1979	64 – F
Cattle Truck, Dodge with regular wheels	1966	37 – D
Cattle Truck, Dodge with SF wheels	1970	37 – E, 71 – F
Celica		
GT, Toyota	1978	25 – H
GT, Toyota with oversized rear wheels	1982	25 – I
Supra, Toyota	1982	39 – F, 60 – G
Cement Mixer	1953	3 – A
Cement Truck		
Albion Chieftain	1958	51 – A
Badger	1976	19 – G
Foden with regular wheels	1968	21 – D
Foden with SF wheels	1970	21 – E
Peterbilt	1982	19 – H
Cherokee, Jeep	1987	27 – H
Chevrolet		
Ambulance Truck	1978	25 – K, 41 – F
Camaro IROC Z	1985	51 – J, SF – 22 – A, LW – 21 – A
Cavalier GS/Opel Vectra	1990	22 – J
Impala	1961	57 – B
Impala Taxi	1965	20 – C
Lumina	1990	54 – I
Chevy Blazer 4x4 Police	1985	50 – H

MODEL DESCRIPTION	YEAR INTRODUCED	MODEL NUMBER(S)
Chevy Van 4x4	1982	44 – G, 68 – E
Chop Suey Motorcycle	1973	49 – D
Chopper, Mission Helicopter	1985	46 – I, 57 – I
Citroen		
CX	1979	12 – G
CX Ambulance	1980	12 – H
DS19	1959	66 – A
15CV	1983	44 – H
SM	1972	51 – E
Claas Combine Harvester	1967	65 – C
Coach		
Airport	1977	65 – E
BEA	1959	58 – A
Bedford Duplé Long Distance	1956	21 – A
Bedford Duplé Long Distance	1958	21 – B
British European Airways	1959	58 – A
Freeman Inter-City Commuter	1970	22 – E
Ikarus Bus	1987	67 – I
Leyland Royal Tiger	1961	40 – B
Mercedes	1965	68 – B
Railway Passenger	1978	44 – F
Royal Tiger	1961	40 – B
Setra	1970	12 – E
Combine Harvester	1978	51 – F
Combine Harvester, Claas	1967	65 – C
Commando Delivery Truck, Dodge	1982	72 – G
Commer		
Ice Cream Canteen	1963	47 – B
Pickup Truck	1958	50 – A
30CWT Nestle's Van	1959	69 – A
Van, 30CWT	1959	69 – A
Commuter		
Freeman Inter-City	1970	22 – E
Mercury with chrome hubs	1968	73 – C
Mercury with SF wheels and flat roof	1970	73 – D
Mercury with SF wheels and raised roof	1972	73 – E
Police, Mercury	1971	55 – F
Concrete Truck		
Foden Ready Mix	1956	26 – A
Foden Ready Mix	1961	26 – B
Foden Ready Mix	1993	26 – K
Container Truck		
Mercedes	1977	42 – F
Volvo	1985	23 – I, 62 – J
Corvette		
Grand Sport	1988	2 – K, 15 – L

MODEL DESCRIPTION	YEAR INTRODUCED	MODEL NUMBER(S)
Hard Top	1983	62 – H
1983 Convertible	1983	14 – I
1984 Convertible	1984	14 – J, SF – 13 – A, LW – 13 – A
1987 Convertible	1987	14 – L
1988 Convertible	1988	14 – M
Pace Car	1983	21 – H
'62 Corvette	1982	71 – G
T-Roof	1982	40 – F, 62 – G
Cosmic Blues	1980	26 – G
Cosmobile	1975	68 – D
Countach, Lamborghini	1973	27 – F
Countach LP500S, Lamborghini	1985	67 – H
Cougar		
Mercury with chrome hubs	1968	62 – C
Mercury with SF wheels	1970	62 – D
Rat Rod, Mercury	1970	62 – E
Villager, Mercury	1978	74 – E
Courier, Ford Van	1992	38 – I
Covered Trailer		
Mercedes with regular wheels	1968	2 – D
Mercedes with SF wheels	1970	2 – E
Covered Truck		
Mercedes with regular wheels	1968	1 – E
Mercedes with SF wheels	1970	1 – F
Volvo	1984	26 – H
Crane		
Iron Fairy with regular wheels	1969	42 – C
Iron Fairy with SF wheels	1970	42 – D
Faun Mobile	1985	42 – H
Taylor Jumbo	1965	11 – C
Crane Truck		
Crane Truck	1976	49 – E
Dodge, 8-Wheel with regular wheels	1968	63 – C
Dodge, 8-Wheel with SF wheels	1970	63 – D
8-Wheel with regular wheels	1965	30 – C
8-Wheel with SF wheels	1970	30 – D
Faun Mobile	1985	42 – H
6-Wheel	1961	30 – B
D		
D-Type Jaguar	1957	41 – A
D-Type Jaguar	1960	41 – B
DAF Girder Truck with regular wheels	1968	58 – C
DAF Girder Truck with SF wheels	1970	58 – D
DAF Tipper Container Truck with regular wheels	1968	47 – C
DAF Tipper Container Truck with SF wheels	1970	47 – D
Daimler Ambulance	1956	14 – A
Daimler Ambulance	1958	14 – B

MODEL DESCRIPTION	YEAR INTRODUCED	MODEL NUMBER(S)
Daimler Bus with regular wheels	1966	74 – B
Daimler Bus with SF wheels	1970	74 – C
Datsun		
126X	1973	33 – E
260Z 2+2	1978	67 – E
280ZX	1982	24 – G
280ZX 2+2	1983	24 – H, SF – 9 – A, LW – 9 – A
Delivery Truck, Dodge Commando	1982	72 – G
Dennis Fire Escape, made in England by Lesney	1955	9 – A
Dennis Fire Escape, made in China	1988	9 – Ja, 9 – Jb
Dennis Refuse Truck	1963	15 – C
Desert Dawg Jeep 4x4	1982	20 – F
DeTomaso Pantera	1975	8 – H
DeTomaso Pantera Greased Lightning	1983	8 – J
Diablo, Lamborghini	1992	22 – K
Diesel Road Roller, made in England by Lesney	1953	1 – A
Diesel Road Roller, made in China	1988	1 – La, 1 – Lb
Diesel Shunter	1978	24 – F
Dodge		
Caravan	1984	64 – G, 68 – F
Cattle Truck with regular wheels	1966	37 – D
Cattle Truck with SF wheels	1970	37 – E, 12 – K, 4 – E
Challenger	1976	1 – H
Challenger/Mitsubishi Galant Eterna	1980	63 – G
Challenger Revin' Rebel	1982	1 – I
Challenger Toyman	1983	1 – J
Charger Mk III	1970	52 – C
Charger Orange Peel Dragster	1981	74 – F
Commando Delivery Truck	1982	72 – G
Crane Truck with regular wheels	1968	63 – C
Crane Truck with SF wheels	1970	63 – D
Dakota Pickup	1989	17 – J, 50 – I
Daytona Turbo Z	1984	28 – I, SF – 4 – A, LW – 4 – A
Delivery Truck	1982	72 – G
Dragster	1971	70 – D
Dump Truck with regular wheels	1966	48 – C
Dump Truck with SF wheels	1970	48 – D
Stake Truck with regular wheels	1967	4 – D
Stake Truck with SF wheels	1970	4 – E, 12 – M
Wreck Truck with regular wheels	1965	13 – D
Wreck Truck with SF wheels	1970	13 – E
Dragon Wheels	1972	43 – E
Draguar, Hot Rod	1970	36 – E
Drott Excavator	1963	58 – B
DUKW Army Amphibian	1959	55 – A
Dump Truck		
AEC 8-Wheel Tipper with regular wheels	1969	51 – C

MODEL DESCRIPTION	YEAR INTRODUCED	MODEL NUMBER(S)
AEC 8-Wheel Tipper with SF wheels	1970	51 – D
Atlas	1975	23 – E
Bedford Tipper Truck	1957	40 – A
Dodge with regular wheels	1966	48 – C
Dodge with SF wheels	1970	48 – D
Earth Mover	1976	9 – K, 53 – H, 58 – F
Faun	1976	9 – K, 53 – H, 58 – F
GMC Tipper Truck with regular wheels	1968	26 – C
GMC Tipper Truck with SF wheels	1970	26 – D
Hoveringham Tipper	1963	17 – C
Laing Muir Hill	1961	2 – C
Mack Dump Truck with regular wheels	1968	28 – D
Mack Dump Truck with SF wheels	1970	28 – E
Muir Hill	1961	2 – C
Site	1976	26 – F
Dune Buggy, Baja	1971	13 – F
Dune Man Volkswagen	1984	49 – G
Dunes Racer 4x4 Mini Pickup	1983	13 – I
Dunlop Bedford 12CWT Van	1956	25 – A

E

MODEL DESCRIPTION	YEAR INTRODUCED	MODEL NUMBER(S)
Earth Mover Faun Dump Truck	1976	9 – K, 53 – H, 58 – F
Eccles Caravan Travel Trailer	1970	57 – E
8-Wheel Truck		
Crane Truck with regular wheels	1965	30 – C
Crane Truck with SF wheels	1970	30 – D
Tipper Truck, AEC with regular wheels	1969	51 – C
Tipper Truck, AEC with SF wheels	1970	51 – D
ERF 686 Truck, "EVEREADY FOR LIFE"	1959	20 – B
Ergomatic Cab AEC Horse Box with regular wheels	1969	17 – D
Ergomatic Cab AEC Horse Box with SF wheels	1970	17 – E
Escort RS2000	1978	9 – F
Escort XR3I Cabriolet	1985	17 – I, SF – 15 – A, LW – 15 – A
Estate Car, Ford Thames	1959	70 – A
Estate Car, Vauxhall Victor	1963	38 – B
"EVEREADY FOR LIFE," ERF 686 Truck	1959	20 – B
Excavator		
Atlas	1981	32 – G
Weatherhill	1956	24 – A
Weatherhill	1959	24 – B
Extending Ladder Fire Engine	1984	18 – H

F

MODEL DESCRIPTION	YEAR INTRODUCED	MODEL NUMBER(S)
Fandango	1975	35 – D
Faun Earth Mover Dump Truck	1976	9 – K, 53 – H, 58 – F
Ferrari		
Berlinetta with chrome hubs or spoked hubs	1965	75 – B
Berlinetta with with SF wheels	1970	75 – C

MODEL DESCRIPTION	YEAR INTRODUCED	MODEL NUMBER(S)
F1 Racer	1962	73 – B
F40	1989	24 – J, 70 – H
Testarossa	1987	75 – G, SF – 24 – A, LW – 23 – A
308 GTB	1981	70 – F, SF – 11 – A, LW – 11 – A
Ferret Scout Car	1959	61 – A
Fiat Abarth	1982	9 – G
Fiat 1500	1965	56 – B
Field Car with yellow or red hubs	1969	18 – E
Field Car with SF wheels	1970	18 – F
Field Gun	1978	32 – F
Fiero	1985	2 – I, SF – 19 – A, LW – 19 – A
'57 Chevy	1979	4 – H
'57 T-Bird	1979	4 – H
Firebird		
Racer, Pontiac	1986	12 – J, SF – 18 – A, LW – 18 – A
S/E, Pontiac	1982	12 – I, 60 – F, SF – 2 – A, LW – 2 – A
S/E, Pontiac	1993	48 – J
Trans Am, Pontiac	1979	16 – F, 16 – G
Fire Chief		
Fire Chief	1976	64 – E
Ford Fairlane	1963	59 – B
Ford Galaxie with regular wheels	1966	59 – C
Ford Galaxie with SF wheels	1970	59 – D
Mercury Parklane	1971	59 – E
Fire Engine		
Airport Fire Tender	1992	24 – L
Blaze Buster	1975	22 – F
Land Rover with regular wheels	1966	57 – C
Land Rover with SF wheels	1970	57 – D
Extending Ladder	1984	18 – H
Merryweather	1959	9 – B
Merryweather	1969	35 – C
Snorkel	1977	13 – G
Snorkel	1982	63 – H
Fire Escape, Dennis, made in England by Lesney	1955	9 – A
Fire Escape, Dennis, made in China	1988	9 – Ja, 9 – Jb
Fire Pumper Truck with regular wheels	1966	29 – C
Fire Pumper Truck with SF wheels	1970	29 – D
Fire Tender, Airport	1992	24 – L
Fire Truck		
Airport Fire Tender	1992	24 – L
Airport Foam Tender	1985	54 – H
Blaze Buster	1975	22 – F
Extending Ladder	1984	18 – H
Land Rover with regular wheels	1966	57 – C

MODEL DESCRIPTION	YEAR INTRODUCED	MODEL NUMBER(S)
Land Rover with SF wheels	1970	57 – D
Merryweather	1959	9 – B
Merryweather	1969	35 – C
Snorkel	1977	13 – G
Snorkel	1982	63 – H
Flame Out	1983	67 – F
Flareside Pickup	1982	53 – Ga
Flareside Pickup, Baja Bouncer	1983	53 – Gb
Flat Car with container	1978	25 – G
Flying Bug	1972	11 – F
Floodlight Heavy Rescue, Mack Power Truck	1991	57 – K
Foam Pumper, Airport Fire Truck	1985	54 – H
Foden		
Concrete Truck with regular wheels	1968	21 – D
Concrete Truck with SF wheels	1970	21 – E
Ready Mix Concrete Truck	1956	26 – A
Ready Mix Concrete Truck	1961	26 – B
Ready Mix Concrete Truck	1993	26 – K
Ford		
Army 3-Ton Service Ambulance	1959	63 – A
Anglia	1961	7 – B
Boss Mustang	1972	44 – B
Bronco II 4x4	1990	39 – H
Capri	1971	54 – D
Capri, Hot Rocker	1973	67 – D
Corsair	1965	45 – B
Cortina GT with regular wheels	1968	25 – D
Cortina GT with SF wheels	1970	25 – E
Cortina 1600 GL	1979	55 – H, 55 – I
Courier Van	1992	38 – I
Customline Station Wagon	1960	31 – B
Escort RS2000	1978	9 – F
Escort XR3i Cabriolet	1985	17 – I, SF – 15 – A, LW – 15 – A
Fairlane Fire Chief	1963	59 – B
Fairlane Police	1963	55 – B
Fairlane Station Wagon	1960	31 – B
'57 T-Bird	1982	42 – G
Galaxie Fire Chief with regular wheels	1966	59 – C
Galaxie Fire Chief with SF wheels	1970	59 – D
Group 6	1970	45 – C
GT with plastic hubs	1965	41 – C
GT with SF wheels	1970	41 – D
Heavy Wreck Truck with regular wheels	1968	71 – C
Heavy Wreck Truck with SF wheels	1970	71 – D
Kennel Truck with regular wheels	1969	50 – C
Kennel Truck with SF wheels	1970	50 – D
LTD Police	1990	16 – J

MODEL DESCRIPTION	YEAR INTRODUCED	MODEL NUMBER(S)
Ford		
LTD Taxi	1992	53 – I
Model A	1979	73 – G
Model A	1980	73 – H
Model A Truck	1982	38 – H
Model T Van, 1921	1990	44 – J
Mustang Boss	1972	44 – E
Mustang Cobra	1982	11 – H
Mustang Fastback with chrome hubs	1966	8 – E
Mustang Fastback with SF wheels	1970	8 – F
Mustang, Good Vibrations	1983	60 – E
Mustang, IMSA	1983	11 – I
Mustang, Piston Popper	1973	10 – F, 60 – E
Mustang Wildcat Dragster	1970	8 – G
Pickup with regular wheels	1968	6 – D
Pickup with SF wheels	1970	6 – E
Prefect	1956	30 – A
Refuse Truck	1966	7 – C
Refuse Truck	1970	7 – D
RS200	1897	34 – J
RS2000 Escort	1978	9 – F
Service Ambulance, Army 3-Ton 4x4	1959	63 – A
Sierra XR4	1983	15 – H, 15 – I, 40 – G, 55 – K, SF – 7 – A, LW – 7 – A
Skip Truck	1988	70 – G
SuperVan II	1985	6 – I, 72 – K
T-Bird	1960	75 – A
T-Bird, 1957	1982	42 – G
T-Bird Turbo Coupe	1988	59 – H, 61 – F
Thames Estate Car	1959	70 – A
Thames Singer Van	1959	59 – A
Thames Trader Wreck Truck	1961	13 – C
Thunderbird	1960	75 – A
Thunderbird, 1957	1982	42 – G
Thunderbird Turbo Coupe	1988	59 – H, 61 – F
3-Ton 4x4 Service Ambulance	1959	63 – A
Tractor	1967	39 – C
Tractor	1978	46 – F
Transit Truck	1977	66 – F
Transit Van	1987	57 – J, 60 – H
Wreck Truck	1978	61 – D
Zephyr 6 Mk III	1963	33 – B
Zodiac Convertible	1957	39 – A
Zodiac Sedan	1957	33 – A
Zodiac Mk IV with regular wheels	1968	53 – C
Zodiac Mk IV with SF wheels	1970	53 – D

MODEL DESCRIPTION	YEAR INTRODUCED	MODEL NUMBER(S)
Fordson Power Major Tractor	1959	72 – A
Fork Lift		
Sambron Jack Lift	1977	48 – F, 28 – M
Truck	1972	15 – G
Truck	1991	28 – M
Formula Racer		
1 Racer	1971	34 – E
1 Racer	1984	6 – H, 16 – H, 28 – H, 65 – G
1 Racer, Team Matchbox	1973	24 – E
1 Racer, Williams Honda Grand Prix	1988	74 – J
5000	1975	36 – F
Racer	1971	34 – E
Racer	1984	6 – H, 16 – H, 28 – H, 65 – G
Racer, Team Matchbox	1973	24 – E
Racer, Williams Honda Grand Prix	1988	74 – J
4 x 4		
Chevy Blazer Police	1985	50 – H
Chevy Van	1982	44 – G
Desert Dawg Jeep	1982	20 – F
Dunes Racer Mini Pickup	1983	13 – I
Golden Eagle Off-Road Jeep	1982	5 – H
Jeep Desert Dawg	1982	20 – F
Jeep Eagle	1983	20 – H
Jeep Golden Eagle	1982	5 – H
Jeep Laredo	1983	20 – H
Mini Pickup	1982	13 – H, 13 – I, 57 – H
Mini Pickup Dunes Racer	1983	13 – I
Mini Pickup Mountain Man	1982	57 – H
Mountain Man Mini Pickup	1982	57 – H
Pickup Camper	1982	57 – H
Freeman Inter-City Commuter Bus	1970	22 – E
Freeman Inter-City Commuter Coach	1970	22 – E
Freeway Gas Tanker	1973	63 – E
Freeway Gas Tanker Trailer	1978	63 – F
Front Loader Tractor, Shovel Nose	1976	29 – F

G

MODEL DESCRIPTION	YEAR INTRODUCED	MODEL NUMBER(S)
Gas Tanker, Freeway	1973	63 – E
Gas Tanker Trailer, Freeway	1978	63 – F
General Service Lorry	1959	62 – A
Girder Truck, DAF, with regular wheels	1968	58 – C
Girder Truck, DAF, with SF wheels	1970	58 – D
GMC		
Dump Truck with regular wheels	1968	26 – C
Dump Truck with SF wheels	1970	26 – D
Refrigerator Truck with regular wheels	1967	44 – C
Refrigerator Truck with SF wheels	1970	44 – D

207

MODEL DESCRIPTION	YEAR INTRODUCED	MODEL NUMBER(S)
Tipper Truck with regular wheels	1968	26 – C
Tipper Truck with SF wheels	1970	26 – D
Wreck Truck	1987	21 – J
Grand Prix, Pontiac with regular wheels	1964	22 – C
Grand Prix, Pontiac with SF wheels	1970	22 – D
Gran Fury Police, Plymouth	1979	10 – G
Greased Lightning DeTomaso Pantera	1983	8 – J
Greyhound Bus with regular wheels	1967	66 – C
Greyhound Bus with SF wheels	1970	66 – D
Grit Spreader, Atkinson with regular wheels	1966	70 – B
Grit Spreader, Atkinson with SF wheels	1970	70 – C
Gruesome Twosome	1971	4 – F

H

MODEL DESCRIPTION	YEAR INTRODUCED	MODEL NUMBER(S)
Hairy Hustler	1971	7 – E
Halftrack Mk III Personnel Carrier	1958	49 – A
Halley's Comet Commemorative Cars		
Chevy Pro Stocker	1986	SF – 12 (1981, 54 – G)
Pontiac Firebird S/E	1986	SF – 2 (1984, 60 – F)
Mercury Parklane Police Car	1986	SF – 1 (1986, 55 – L)
Harley Davidson		
Motorcycle	1980	50 – G
Motorcycle and Sidecar	1962	66 – B
Motorcycle, Hondarora	1975	18 – G
Harvester, Combine	1978	51 – F
Harvester, Combine, Claas	1967	65 – C
Hatra Tractor Shovel	1965	69 – B
Hay Trailer	1967	40 – C
Helicopter	1982	75 – F
Helicopter, Mission Chopper	1985	46 – I, 57 – I
Helicopter, Seasprite	1977	75 – E
Hellraiser	1975	55 – G
Highway Maintenance Truck, Mack	1990	69 – I
Hi Ho Silver Volkswagen	1971	15 – F
Hi-Trailer Team Matchbox Racer	1973	24 – E, 56 – D
Holden Ruff Trek Pickup	1983	58 – G
Honda CB750 Police Motorcycle	1977	33 – F
Honda F1 Grand Prix Racer	1988	74 – J
Hot Rocker Ford Capri	1973	67 – D
Hovercraft	1976	2 – G
Hovercraft SRN6	1972	72 – D
Hoveringham Tipper	1963	17 – C

I

MODEL DESCRIPTION	YEAR INTRODUCED	MODEL NUMBER(S)
Ice Cream Truck, Commer	1963	47 – B
Ikarus Bus	1987	67 – I
Impala, Chevrolet	1961	57 – B

MODEL DESCRIPTION	YEAR INTRODUCED	MODEL NUMBER(S)
Impala Taxi, Chevrolet	1965	20 – C
IMSA Mazda	1983	6 – G
IMSA Mustang	1983	11 – I
Indy Racer	1984	65 – G
Inter-City Commuter Coach, Freeman	1970	22 – E
Iron Fairy Crane with regular wheels	1969	42 – C
Iron Fairy Crane with SF wheels	1970	42 – D
Iso Grifo with chrome hubs	1968	14 – D
Iso Grifo with SF wheels	1970	14 – E
Isuzu Amigo	1991	52 – G

J

Jaguar		
D-Type	1957	41 – A
D-Type	1960	41 – B
Mark 10	1964	28 – C
SS100	1982	47 – G
3.4 Litre	1959	65 – A
3.8 Litre	1962	65 – B
XJ220	1993	31 – M
XJ6	1987	1 – K, 41 – I
XJ6 Police	1991	1 – K
XK120	1984	22 – H
XK140	1957	32 – A
XK140	1993	32 – I
XKE	1962	32 – B
Javelin AMX	1971	9 – E

Jeep		
Cherokee, Jeep	1987	27 – H
CJ5	1982	5 – H
CJ5 with separate wheels hubs	1966	72 – B
CJ5 with SF wheels	1970	72 – C
CJ6	1977	53 – F
Desert Dawg	1982	20 – F
Eagle/Laredo	1983	14 – K, 20 – G, 20 – H, 37 – J
4x4 Desert Dawg	1982	20 – F
4x4 Golden Eagle	1982	5 – H
4x4 Laredo/Eagle	1983	14 – K, 20 – G, 20 – H, 37 – J
4x4 Off-Road	1982	20 – F
Gladiator Pickup Truck	1964	71 – B
Hot Rod	1971	2 – F
Sleet -N- Snow U.S. Mail	1978	5 – G
Standard CJ5 with separate hubs	1966	72 – B
U.S. Mail	1978	5 – G
Jet, S-2	1981	2 – H
Jet, Swing Wing	1981	27 – G
John Deere Tractor	1964	50 – B

MODEL DESCRIPTION	YEAR INTRODUCED	MODEL NUMBER(S)
John Deere Trailer	1964	51 – B
Jumbo Crane, Taylor	1965	11 – C
Jumbo Jet Motorcycle	1973	71 – E

K

MODEL DESCRIPTION	YEAR INTRODUCED	MODEL NUMBER(S)
Karrier Refuse Truck	1957	38 – A
Kennel Truck, Ford with regular wheels	1969	50 – C
Kennel Truck, Ford with SF wheels	1970	50 – D
Kenworth Cabover Aerodyne	1982	45 – E
Kenworth Conventional Aerodyne	1982	41 – G

L

MODEL DESCRIPTION	YEAR INTRODUCED	MODEL NUMBER(S)
Laing Muir Hill Dumper	1961	2 – C
Lamborghini		
Countach	1973	27 – F
Countach LP500S	1985	67 – H
Diablo	1991	22 – K
Marzal	1969	20 – D
Miura with chrome hubs	1969	33 – C
Miura with SF wheels	1970	33 – D
Lambretta TV175 Scooter and Sidecar	1961	36 – B
Land Rover		
Land Rover	1955	12 – A
Land Rover	1959	12 – B
Fire Truck with regular wheels	1966	57 – C
Fire Truck with SF wheels	1970	57 – D
Ninety	1990	16 – K, 35 – I
Safari with regular wheels	1965	12 – C
Safari with SF wheels	1970	12 – D
Laredo, 4x4 Jeep	1983	20 – G, 20 – H
LeSabre, Buick	1987	10 – H
Leyland		
Petrol Tanker with regular wheels	1968	32 – C
Petrol Tanker with SF wheels	1970	32 – D
Pipe Truck with regular wheels	1966	10 – D
Pipe Truck with SF wheels	1970	10 – E
Royal Tiger Coach	1961	40 – B
Site Office Truck with regular wheels	1966	60 – B
Site Office Truck with SF wheels	1970	60 – C
Tanker	1982	14 – H
Titan London Bus	1972	17 – F
Titan London Bus	1982	17 – G, 28 – K, 51 – H
Lincoln		
Continental with regular wheels	1964	31 – C
Continental with SF wheels	1969	31 – D
Continental Mark V	1979	28 – G
Town Car	1989	43 – K

MODEL DESCRIPTION	YEAR INTRODUCED	MODEL NUMBER(S)
Locomotive, Pannier Tank	1979	47 – F
Locomotive, 0-4-0 Steam	1978	43 – F
London		
Bus	1954	5 – A
Bus	1957	5 – B
Bus	1961	5 – C
Bus	1965	5 – D
Bus, Leyland Titan	1972	17 – F
Bus, Leyland Titan	1982	17 – G, 28 – K, 51 – H
Bus, The Londoner	1982	17 – G, 28 – K, 51 – H
Taxi, Austin	1987	4 – I
Taxi, Austin	1960	17 – B
Trolley Bus	1959	56 – A
Long Distance Coach, Bedford Duplé	1956	21 – A
Long Distance Coach, Bedford Duplé	1958	21 – B
Lotus		
Europa	1969	5 – E
Racing Car with plastic hubs or spoked wheels	1966	19 – D
Racing Car with SF wheels	1970	19 – E
Super Seven	1971	60 – D
Low Loader, Bedford	1956	27 – A
Low Loader, Bedford	1959	27 – B
Lumina Stock Car	1990	54 – I

M

MODEL DESCRIPTION	YEAR INTRODUCED	MODEL NUMBER(S)
Mack		
Auxiliary Power Truck	1991	57 – K
CH600	1990	8 – M
Dump Truck with regular wheels	1968	28 – D
Dump Truck with SF wheels	1970	28 – E
Floodlight Heavy Rescue Power Truck	1991	57 – K
Mark 10 Jaguar	1964	28 – C
Marshall Horse Box	1957	35 – A
Marzal, Lamborghini	1969	20 – D
Maserati		
Bora	1972	32 – E
Bora Sunburner	1982	37 – H
4CL T/1948	1958	52 – A
Massey Harris Tractor with fenders	1954	4 – A
Massey Harris Tractor without fenders	1957	4 – B
Matra Rancho	1982	37 – I
Maxi Taxi Ford Capri	1973	72 – E
Mazda		
Mazda, IMSA	1983	6 – G
Mazda RX-500	1971	66 – E
Mazda Savannah RX7	1979	31 – G
Mazda RX7	1982	31 – H

MODEL DESCRIPTION	YEAR INTRODUCED	MODEL NUMBER(S)
Mechanical Horse and Trailer	1955	10 – A
Mechanical Horse and Trailer	1958	10 – B
Mercedes Benz		
Ambulance with regular wheels	1968	3 – C
Ambulance with SF wheels	1970	3 – D
Binz Ambulance with regular wheels	1968	3 – C
Binz Ambulance with SF wheels	1970	3 – D
Covered Trailer with regular wheels	1968	2 – D
Covered Trailer with SF wheels	1970	2 – E
Covered Truck with regular wheels	1968	1 – E
Covered Truck with SF wheels	1970	1 – F
500SEC, AMG	1984	43 – I
500SL	1990	12 – L, 33 – K
450SEL	1979	56 – E
450SEL Taxi	1980	56 – F
Lorry with regular wheels	1968	1 – E
Lorry with SF wheels	1970	1 – F
600SL	1992	37 – M
1600 Turbo Tractor	1990	73 – I
300E	1987	58 – H
300SE with regular wheels	1968	46 – C
300SE with SF wheels	1970	46 – D
350SL Convertible	1973	6 – F
Tractor 1600 Turbo	1990	73 – I
220SE	1963	53 – B
220SL Convertible with regular wheels	1966	28 – D
220SL Convertible with SF wheels	1970	28 – E
280GE G-Wagon	1984	30 – I
Mercedes		
Coach	1965	68 – B
Container Truck	1977	42 – F
Covered Trailer with regular wheels	1968	2 – D
Covered Trailer with SF wheels	1970	2 – E
Tractor 1600 Turbo	1990	73 – I
Scaffold Truck with regular wheels	1968	11 – D
Scaffold Truck with SF wheels	1970	11 – E
TV News Truck	1989	68 – H
Unimog	1984	48 – H
Unimog with plastic hubs	1967	49 – B
Unimog with SF wheels	1970	49 – C
Mercury		
Commuter with chrome hubs	1968	73 – C
Commuter with SF wheels and flat roof	1970	73 – D
Commuter with SF wheels and raised roof	1972	73 – E
Commuter Police	1971	55 – F
Cougar with chrome hubs	1968	62 – C

MODEL DESCRIPTION	YEAR INTRODUCED	MODEL NUMBER(S)
Cougar with SF wheels	1970	62 – D
Cougar Rat Rod	1970	62 – E
Cougar Villager	1978	74 – E
Parklane Fire Chief	1971	59 – E
Parklane Police with chrome hubs	1968	55 – D
Parklane Police with SF wheels	1970	55 – E, 55 – K
Sable Wagon	1988	33 – I, 55 – M
Merryweather Fire Engine	1959	9 – B
Merryweather Fire Engine	1969	35 – C
Meteor Sports Boat and Trailer	1958	48 – A
MG		
MG 1100 with regular wheels	1966	64 – B
MG 1100 with SF wheels	1970	64 – C
MG Midget Sports Car	1956	19 – A
MG Midget Sports Car	1993	19 – I
MGA Sports Car	1958	19 – B
Midnight Magic	1982	51 – G
Military Tank	1993	70 – I
Milk		
Delivery Van, Bedford	1956	29 – A
Delivery Van, Commer	1961	21 – C
Float, Horse Drawn	1954	7 – A
Float, Horse Drawn	1988	7 – K
Truck, Bedford	1956	29 – A
Truck, Commer	1961	21 – C
Mini		
HaHa Mini Cooper	1975	14 – G
Pickup Camper	1982	22 – G
Pickup 4x4	1982	13 – H, 13 – I
Mission Chopper	1985	46 – I, 57 - I
Mitsubishi Galant Eterna/Dodge Challenger	1980	63 – G
Mobile Canteen Refreshment Bar	1959	74 – A
Mobile Crane, Faun	1985	42 – H
Mod Rod	1971	1 – G
Model A Ford	1979	73 – G
Model A Ford	1980	73 – H
Model A Ford Truck	1982	38 – H
Model T Ford Van, 1921	1990	44 – J
Modified Racer	1990	32 – H
Monteverdi Hai	1973	3 – E
Morris J2 Pickup	1959	60 – A
Morris Minor 1000	1958	46 – A
Motor Home	1980	54 – F
Motorcycle and Sidecar, Harley Davidson	1962	66 – B
Motorcycle and Sidecar, Triumph	1960	4 – C
Motorcycle		
Chop Suey	1973	49 – D

MODEL DESCRIPTION	YEAR INTRODUCED	MODEL NUMBER(S)
Harley Davidson	1980	50 – G
Harley Davidson, Hondarora	1975	18 – G
Hondarora Harley Davidson	1975	18 – G
Jumbo Jet	1973	71 – E
Moving Van, Pickford Removals	1960	46 – B
Mustang		
Cobra	1982	11 – H
Fastback with chrome hubs	1966	8 – E
Fastback with SF wheels	1970	8 – F
GT350	1979	23 – F
IMSA	1983	11 – I
Piston Popper	1973	10 – F, 60 - E

N

MODEL DESCRIPTION	YEAR INTRODUCED	MODEL NUMBER(S)
1921 Model T Ford Van	1990	44 – J
1933 Willy's Street Rod	1982	69 – G
1962 Corvette	1982	71 – G
1983 Corvette Convertible	1983	14 – I
1984 Corvette Convertible	1984	14 – J
1984 Dodge Daytona Turbo Z	1984	28 – I, SF – 4 – A
1987 Corvette Convertible	1987	14 – L
1987 Nissan 300ZX	1987	24 – I
1988 Corvette Convertible	1988	14 – M
1990 Nissan 300ZX	1990	37 – L, 61 – G
NASA Rocket Transporter	1985	40 – H, 60 – I
NASA Tracking Vehicle	1982	54 – G
New Ford Transit Van	1987	57 – J, 60 – H
Nissan 300ZX	1990	37 – L, 61 – G
Nissan 300ZX Turbo	1987	24 – I
Nissan Prairie	1991	21 – K, 31 – L

O

MODEL DESCRIPTION	YEAR INTRODUCED	MODEL NUMBER(S)
Oldsmobile Aerotech	1989	62 – L
Opel Diplomat with regular wheels	1966	36 – C
Opel Diplomat with SF wheels	1970	36 – D
Opel Kadet/Vauxhall Astra Police	1987	8 – L
Opel Vectra/Chevrolet Cavalier GS	1990	22 – J
Orange Peel Dodge Charger	1981	74 – F

P

MODEL DESCRIPTION	YEAR INTRODUCED	MODEL NUMBER(S)
Pannier Tank Locomotive	1979	47 – F
Pantera, DeTomaso	1975	8 – H
Pantera, DeTomaso, Greased Lightning	1983	8 – J
Passenger Coach, Railway	1978	44 – F
Personnel Carrier		
Personnel Carrier	1976	54 – E
Army Halftrack Mk III	1958	49 – A
Army Saracen	1959	54 – A

MODEL DESCRIPTION	YEAR INTRODUCED	MODEL NUMBER(S)
Peterbilt		
Cement Truck	1982	19 – H
Conventional	1982	43 – H
Dump Truck	1982	30 – H
Petrol Tanker	1982	5 – I, 56 – G
Quarry Truck	1982	30 – H
Tanker	1982	5 – I, 56 – G
Wreck Truck	1982	61 – E
Petrol Tanker		
Leyland with regular wheels	1968	32 – C
Leyland with SF wheels	1970	32 – D
Peterbilt	1982	5 – I, 56 – G
Peugeot Quasar	1985	25 – L, 49 – H
Peugeot 205 Turbo 16	1985	15 – J
Pickford Removal Van	1960	46 – B
Pickup Camper, 4x4	1986	35 – G, 38 – G
Pickup Truck		
Commer	1958	50 – A
Holden Ruff Trek	1983	58 – G
Jeep Gladiator	1964	71 – B
Morris J2	1959	60 – A
Pi-Eyed Piper	1972	48 – E
Pipe Truck, Leyland with regular wheels	1966	10 – D
Pipe Truck, Leyland with SF wheels	1970	10 – E
Piston Popper Ford Mustang	1973	10 – F, 60 – E
Planet Scout	1975	59 – F
Plymouth Gran Fury Police	1979	10 – G
Police		
Blazer 4x4	1985	50 – H
Chevrolet Blazer 4x4	1985	50 – H
Ford Fairlane	1963	55 – B
Ford Galaxie	1966	55 – C
Ford LTD	1990	16 – J
Gran Fury	1979	10 – G
Launch	1976	52 – D
LTD	1990	16 – J
Mercury Commuter	1971	55 – F
Mercury Parklane with chrome hubs	1968	55 – D
Mercury Parklane with SF wheels	1970	55 – E
Motorcyclist	1977	33 – F
Patrol, Range Rover, Rolamatic	1979	20 – E
Plymouth Gran Fury	1979	10 – G
Pontiac		
Convertible	1962	39 – B
Fiero	1985	2 – I
Firebird Racer	1986	12 – J
Firebird S/E	1982	12 – I

MODEL DESCRIPTION	YEAR INTRODUCED	MODEL NUMBER(S)
Firebird S/E	1993	48 – J
Firebird Trans Am	1979	16 – F
Firebird Trans Am	1982	16 – G
Firebird Trans Am T-Roof	1982	16 – I, 35 – F
Grand Prix with regular wheels	1964	22 – C
Grand Prix with SF wheels	1970	22 – D
Stock Car	1993	35 – J
Trans Am	1979	16 – F
Trans Am	1982	16 – G
Trans Am T-Roof	1982	16 – I, 35 – F
Pony Trailer with regular wheels	1968	43 – C
Pony Trailer with SF wheels	1970	43 – D
Porsche		
910	1970	68 – C
911 Turbo	1978	3 – F
928	1980	59 – G
935, Super Porsche Racer	1983	55 – J
944	1988	71 – I
959	1987	7 – J
Turbo 911	1978	3 – F
Portland Cement Truck, Albion Chieftain	1958	51 – A
Pressure Refueling Tanker, RAF 10-Ton	1959	73 – A
Prime Mover Truck Tractor	1956	15 – A
Pro Stocker, Chevy	1981	34 – G
Pro Stocker, Chevy, Halley's Comet	1986	34 – I, SF – 12 – B

Q

MODEL DESCRIPTION	YEAR INTRODUCED	MODEL NUMBER(S)
Quarry Truck		
Quarry Truck	1954	6 – A
Quarry Truck	1993	6 – K
Earth Mover	1976	9 – K, 53 – H, 58 – F
Euclid	1957	6 – B
Euclid	1964	6 – C
Faun Dump Truck	1976	9 – K, 53 – H, 58 – F
Peterbilt	1982	30 – H
Quasar, Peugeot	1985	49 – H, 25 – L

R

MODEL DESCRIPTION	YEAR INTRODUCED	MODEL NUMBER(S)
Racer		
BRM	1965	52 – B
Formula	1984	6 – H, 16 – H, 28 – H, 65 – G
Formula 1	1971	34 – E
Formula 1	1984	6 – H, 16 – H, 28 – H, 65 – G
Formula, Team Matchbox	1973	24 – E
Indy	1984	6 – H, 16 – H, 28 – H, 65 – G
Modified	1990	32 – H
Sprint	1990	34 – K

MODEL DESCRIPTION	YEAR INTRODUCED	MODEL NUMBER(S)
Super Porsche 935	1983	55 – J
Team Matchbox Formula 1	1973	24 – E
Racing Mini	1970	29 – E
Radio Truck, Austin Mk 2	1959	68 – A
RAF 10-Ton Pressure Refueling Tanker	1959	73 – A
Railway Passenger Coach	1978	44 – F
Rallye Royale	1973	14 – F
Range Rover Police Patrol	1975	20 – E
Rat Rod Mercury Cougar	1970	62 – E
Ready Mix Concrete Truck, Foden	1956	26 – A
Ready Mix Concrete Truck, Foden	1961	26 – B
Red Rider	1982	48 – G
Refrigerator Truck, GMC with regular wheels	1967	44 – C
Refrigerator Truck, GMC with SF wheels	1970	44 – D
Refueling Tanker, RAF 10-Ton Pressure	1959	73 – A
Refuse Truck		
Refuse Truck	1980	36 – G
Dennis	1963	15 – C
Karrier	1957	38 – A
Removal Van, Bedford	1956	17 – A
Removal Van, Pickford	1960	46 – B
Renault		
5TL	1978	21 – G
17TL	1974	62 – F
11 Turbo Alliance	1987	43 – J
Revin' Rebel Dodge Challenger	1982	1 – I
Road Dragster	1970	19 – F
Road Roller		
Road Roller	1953	1 – A
Road Roller	1955	1 – B
Road Roller	1958	1 – C
Aveling Barford	1962	1 – D
Bomag	1979	40 – I, 72 – F
Diesel	1953	1 – A
Diesel	1988	1 – L
Road Tanker	1955	11 – A
Road Tanker	1958	11 – B
Rocket Transporter, NASA	1985	40 – H, 60 – I
Rod Roller	1973	21 – F
Rolls Royce		
Phantom V	1964	44 – B
Silver Cloud	1958	44 – A
Silver Cloud	1985	31 – I, 62 – I
Silver Shadow with chrome hubs	1967	24 – C
Silver Shadow with SF wheels	1970	24 – D
Silver Shadow Convertible Coupe	1969	69 – C
Silver Shadow II	1979	39 – E

MODEL DESCRIPTION	YEAR INTRODUCED	MODEL NUMBER(S)
Silver Spirit	1990	55 – N
Rompin' Rabbit VW	1982	7 – G
Rover Sterling	1988	31 – J
Rover 3500 Police	1982	8 – I
Royal Tiger Coach, Leyland	1961	40 – B
Ruff Rabbit VW	1983	7 – H
Ruff Trek Holden Pickup	1983	58 – G
RX-7 Mazda Savannah	1979	31 – G
RX-7 Mazda	1982	31 – H

S

MODEL DESCRIPTION	YEAR INTRODUCED	MODEL NUMBER(S)
6 -Wheel Crane	1961	30 – B
S-2 Jet	1981	2 – H
Saab 9000	1988	15 – K
Saab Sonnet	1973	65 – D
Safari Land Rover with regular wheels	1965	12 – C
Safari Land Rover with SF wheels	1970	12 – D
Saladin Armoured Car	1959	67 – A
Sambron Jack Lift	1977	48 F, 28 – M
Sand Digger VW	1983	49 – F
Sand Racer	1984	72 – H
Saracen Personnel Carrier	1959	54 – A
Sauber Group C Racer	1985	66 – H
Savannah RX-7 Mazda	1979	31 – G
Scaffold Truck, Mercedes with regular wheels	1969	11 – D
Scaffold Truck, Mercedes with SF wheels	1970	11 – E
Scammell Breakdown Truck	1959	64 – A
Scammell Mountaineer	1964	16 – C
Scania T142	1986	8 – K, 71 – H
School Bus	1985	47 – H
Scout Cat, Ferret	1959	61 – A
Seafire Boat	1975	5 – F
Seasprite Helicopter	1977	75 – E
Self-Propelled Gun	1976	70 – E
Service Ambulance Ford 3-Ton 4x4	1959	63 – A
Setra Coach	1970	12 – E
Shovel Nose Tractor	1976	29 – F
Shunter Diesel	1978	24 – F
Sierra XR4	1983	15 – H, 15 – I, 40 – G, 55 – K, SF – 7 – A
Silver Cloud, Rolls Royce	1958	44 – A
Silver Cloud, Rolls Royce	1985	31 – I, 62 – I
Silver Shadow, Rolls Royce with chrome hubs	1967	24 – C
Silver Shadow, Rolls Royce with SF wheels	1970	24 – D
Silver Shadow Convertible Coupe, Rolls Royce	1969	69 – C
Silver Shadow II, Rolls Royce	1979	39 – E

MODEL DESCRIPTION	YEAR INTRODUCED	MODEL NUMBER(S)
Silver Spirit, Rolls Royce	1990	55 – N
Singer Ford Thames Van	1959	59 – A
Site Dumper	1976	26 – F
Site Office Truck, Leyland with regular wheels	1966	60 – B
Site Office Truck, Leyland with SF wheels	1970	60 – C
Siva Spider	1972	41 – E
Skip Truck	1976	37 – G
Skip Truck, Ford	1988	70 – G
Skoda 130LR Rally	1988	44 – I
Sleet -N- Snow U.S. Mail Jeep	1978	5 – G
Slingshot Dragster	1971	64 – D
Snorkel Fire Engine	1982	63 – H
Snorkel Fire Engine	1977	13 – G
Snowplow, Chevrolet Highway Maintenance	1990	45 – G, 69 – I
SnowTrac Tractor	1964	35 – B
Soopa Coopa	1972	37 – F
Sports Boat and Trailer	1961	48 – B
Sports Boat and Trailer, Meteor	1958	48 – A
Sprint Racer	1990	34 – K
Stake Truck	1956	20 – A
Stake Truck, Dodge with regular wheels	1967	4 – D
Stake Truck, Dodge with SF wheels	1970	4 – E
Standard Jeep CJ5 with plastic hubs	1962	72 – B
Standard Jeep CJ5 with SF wheels	1970	72 – C
Steam Locomotive 0-4-0	1978	43 – F
Sterling Rover	1988	2 – J, 31 – J
Stingeroo Cycle	1973	38 – E
Stoat Armored Truck	1974	28 – F
Stretcha Fetcha	1972	46 – E
Studebaker Lark Wagonaire	1965	42 – B
Sugar Container Truck	1961	10 – C
Sunburner	1992	15 – N
Sunburner Maserati Bora	1982	37 – H
Super Porsche 935 Racer	1983	55 – J
Superboss, Tyrone Malone Competition Truck	1982	66 – G
Supervan II, Ford	1985	6 – I, 72 – K
Swamp Rat Airboat	1976	30 – F
Swing Wing Jet	1981	27 – G

T

T-Bird	1960	75 – A
T-Bird, '57	1982	42 – G
T-Bird Stock Car	1993	7 – L
T-Bird Turbo Coupe	1988	59 – H, 61 – F
Tank , Locomotive, Pannier	1979	47 – F
Tanker		
Bedford Petrol	1964	25 – C

MODEL DESCRIPTION	YEAR INTRODUCED	MODEL NUMBER(S)
Freeway Gas	1973	63 – E
Leyland Patrol with regular wheels	1968	32 – C
Leyland Patrol with SF wheels	1970	32 – D
Peterbilt	1982	5 – I, 56 – G
Tanker Trailer, Freeway Gas	1978	63 – F
Tanzara	1972	53 – E
Taxi		
Austin	1960	17 – B
Austin	1987	4 – I
Capri Maxi Taxi	1973	72 – E
Chevrolet Impala	1965	20 – C
Ford Capri Maxi Taxi	1973	72 – E
Ford LTD	1992	53 – I
Impala	1965	20 – C
Maxi Taxi	1973	72 – E
Mercedes Benz 450SEL	1980	56 – F
Mercedes Capri Maxi Taxi	1973	72 – E
Taylor Jumbo Crane	1965	11 – C
Team Matchbox Formula 1 Racer	1973	24 – E
Team Matchbox Hi-Tailer Formula 1 Racer	1974	56 – D
Thames Trader Compressor Truck	1959	28 – B
Thames Trader Wreck Truck	1961	13 – C
Tilt Truck, Volvo Covered	1984	26 – H
Tipper Container Truck, DAF with regular wheels	1968	47 – C
Tipper Container Truck, DAF with SF wheels	1970	47 – D
Tipper Truck		
AEC 8-Wheel with regular wheels	1969	51 – C
AEC 8-Wheel with SF wheels	1970	51 – D
Atlas	1975	23 – E
Bedford	1957	40 – A
GMC with regular wheels	1968	26 – C
GMC with SF wheels	1970	26 – D
Hoveringham	1963	17 – C
Toe Joe Wrecker	1972	74 – D
Toyman Dodge Challenger	1983	1 – J
Toyota		
Celica GT	1978	25 – H
Celica GT	1982	25 – I
Celica Supra	1982	39 – F, 60 – G
MR2	1987	9 – I, SF – 23 – A
Mini Pickup Camper	1982	22 – G
Tractor		
Ford	1967	39 – C
Ford	1978	46 – F
Fordson Power Major	1959	72 – A
John Deere	1964	50 – B

MODEL DESCRIPTION	YEAR INTRODUCED	MODEL NUMBER(S)
Massey Harris	1954	4 – A
Massey Harris	1957	4 – B
Massey Harris	1988	4 – J
Mod	1972	25 – F
Tractor Shovel, Aveling Barford	1962	43 – B
Tractor Shovel, Hatra	1965	69 – B
Trailer		
Caravan	1965	23 – C
Caravan Travel	1977	31 – F
Eccles Caravan Travel	1970	57 – E
John Deere	1964	51 – B
Trans Am, Pontiac	1979	16 – F, 16 – G, 16 – I, 35 – F
Transporter		
Airplane	1985	72 – I
Bedford Car	1976	11 – G
NASA Rocket	1985	40 – H, 60 – I
Rescue Plane	1985	72 – I
Travel Trailer		
Berkeley Cavalier	1956	23 – A
Bluebird Dauphine	1960	23 – B
Caravan	1965	23 – C
Caravan	1977	31 – F
Eccles Caravan	1970	57 – E
Triumph Motorcycle and Sidecar	1960	4 – C
Trojan 1-Ton Van Brooke Bond Tea	1958	47 – A
Trolley Bus, London	1959	56 – A
Turbo Fury	1973	69 – D
TV News Truck	1989	68 – H
TV Service Van	1963	62 – B
Tyre Fryer	1972	42 – E
Tyrone Malone Bandag Bandit	1982	65 – F
Tyrone Malone Super Boss	1982	66 – G

U

MODEL DESCRIPTION	YEAR INTRODUCED	MODEL NUMBER(S)
U.S. Mail Jeep	1978	5 – G
Unimog with plastic hubs	1967	49 – B
Unimog with SF wheels	1967	49 – C
Unimog with plow	1984	48 – H
Utility Truck, Ford	1989	33 – J

V

MODEL DESCRIPTION	YEAR INTRODUCED	MODEL NUMBER(S)
Van		
Bedford Matchbox Removal Service	1956	17 – A
Bedford 12CWT Dunlop	1956	25– A
Bedford Evening News	1957	42 – A
Chevy	1979	68 – E
Chevy 4x4	1982	44 – G
Commer 30CWT Nestle's	1959	69– A

MODEL DESCRIPTION	YEAR INTRODUCED	MODEL NUMBER(S)
Commer Ice Cream Canteen	1963	47 – B
Ford 1921 Model T	1990	44 – J
Ford Thames Singer	1959	59 – A
Ford Transit	1990	57 – J
Pickford Removal	1960	46 – B
Trojan 1-Ton Brooke Bond Tea	1958	47 – A
Thames Singer	1959	59 – A
Vantastic	1975	34 – F
Vauxhall		
Astra GTE	1987	48 – I
Astra/Opel Kadet Police	1987	8 – L
Cresta	1956	22 – A
Cresta	1958	22 – B
Guildsman	1971	40 – D
Victor Estate Car	1963	38 – B
Victor Sedan	1958	45 – A
Volks Dragon	1971	31 – E
Volkswagen		
1200	1960	25 – B
1500 Saloon with chrome hubs	1968	15 – D
1500 Saloon with SF wheels	1970	15 – E
1600TL with chrome hubs	1967	67 – B
1600TL with SF wheels	1970	67 – C
Ambulance Vanagon	1988	20 – J
Big Blue	1983	46 – H
Camper	1970	23 – D
Camper with skywindow	1962	34 – B
Camper with raised windowed roof	1967	34 – C
Camper with low, windowless roof	1968	34 – D
Dune Man	1984	49 – G
Flying Bug	1972	11 – F
Golf	1976	7 – F
Golf GTI	1986	33 – G
Hi Ho Silver	1971	15 – F
Hot Chocolate	1982	46 – G
Matchbox Express Van	1957	34 – A
Rabbit	1976	7 – F
Rompin' Rabbit	1982	7 – G
Ruff Rabbit	1983	7 – H
Sand Digger	1983	49 – F
Volvo		
480ES	1989	69 – H
760	1985	62 – K
Cable Truck	1984	26 – I
Container Truck	1985	23 – I, 62 – I
Covered Tilt Truck	1984	26 – H

MODEL DESCRIPTION	YEAR INTRODUCED	MODEL NUMBER(S)
Tilt Truck	1984	26 – H
Zoo Truck	1981	35 – E
W		
Weasel Armored Vehicle	1974	73 – F
Weatherhill Hydraulic Excavator	1956	24 – A
Weatherhill Hydraulic Excavator	1959	24 – B
Wells Fargo Armored Truck	1978	69 – E
Wildlife Truck	1973	57 – F
Williams Honda F1 Grand Prix Racer	1988	74 – J
Willys Street Rod 1933	1982	69 – G
Wolseley 1500	1959	57 – A
Woosh -N- Push	1972	58 – E
Wreck Truck		
Bedford	1955	13 – A
Bedford	1958	13 – B
Bedford	1993	13 – J
Breakdown Van	1986	21 – I
Dodge with regular wheels	1965	13 – D
Dodge with SF wheels	1970	13 – E
Ford	1978	61 – D
Ford Heavy with regular wheels	1968	71 – C
Ford Heavy with SF wheels	1970	71 – D
GMC	1987	21 – J
Peterbilt	1982	61 – E
Scammell Breakdown Truck	1959	64 – A
Thames Trader	1961	13 – C
Toe Joe	1972	74 – D
Wrecker		
Bedford	1955	13 – A
Bedford	1958	13 – B
Breakdown Van	1986	21 – I
Dodge with regular wheels	1965	13 – D
Dodge with SF wheels	1970	13 – E
Ford	1978	61 – D
Ford Heavy with regular wheels	1968	71 – C
Ford Heavy with SF wheels	1970	71 – D
GMC	1987	21 – J
Peterbilt	1982	61 – E
Scammell Breakdown Truck	1959	64 – A
Thames Trader	1961	13 – C
Toe Joe	1972	74 – D
X, Y, Z		
0-4-0 (Zero-Four-Zero) Steam Locomotive	1978	43 – F
Zoo Truck, Volvo	1981	35 – E

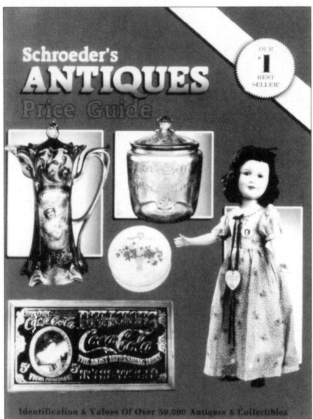